INTENTIONAL MENTORING

DR. KENNETH D. DAVIS, Ed.D.

ISBN: 978-1-957551-03-6

Cover/Interior Design: Bledsoe Publishing Company LLC

Published by: Bledsoe Publishing Company LLC

Printed in the United States of America

FOREWORD

Intentional Mentoring, A Call for Action, is not just another book about mentoring. It is a book about authentic strategies to help mentors connect positively with potential leaders. It is especially helpful for those working with children of color from backgrounds of poverty. I extend my gratitude to Ken for creating this record of what works.

It is a privilege to write this foreword for Ken Davis; his passion for children and his successful record in mentoring the individuals that lead our schools are remarkable. As a principal, he took every advantage of the opportunities to advance his campuses to high levels of achievement and watching him progress over the years has been rewarding. Ken's growth from principal to Area Superintendent to Executive Director of Equity and Outreach is validation that given guidance and support, leaders can develop and impact student success. The strategies in this book provide guidance to ensure that mentoring tools for contemporary educational leadership are not lost, that others will have so much more than a theoretical blueprint for inspiring educators this century.

Serving as a superintendent for 26 years, I saw the need to pass on generational wisdom to new leaders as they influenced those they supervised. Trial and error are not a good method to learn leadership skills in the educational system. Our students do not have the luxury of repeating grades over and over until administrators and teachers get it right. These pages contain strategies that have worked in today's world - in a society demanding more accountability, while that very society is in upheaval. This is exactly why this book is not just valuable, but necessary.

Thomas E. Randle, Ed.D.

Thomas E. Randle & Associates

ACKNOWLEDGMENT

With a heavy heart and joyful jubilation, I smile through tears for those that have been so patient with me through this endeavor. First, I would like to thank the participants for this study. Without their trust, honesty, and patience, this study would not have been possible. Thanks to each one of you for your willingness to extend an olive branch for our children, who so desperately need each one of us to move forward successfully.

I want to thank my dissertation chair, Dr. Sandra L. Harris. Your commitment and patience have been outstanding. You have been with me through the late hours and early mornings, long weekends, and even holidays to support my writing. Thank you from the depths of my soul for your support, kindness, and respectful candor.

Thank you too, committee members, Dr. Johnny O'Connor, Jr., and Dr. Brett C. Welch. Your support and critiques have shaped my writing, ideas, and molded more of my expertise for children.

Thank you to my sons, Jarvis and Marcus. They have been extremely patient with me while they have sacrificed many nights, weekends, holiday, school events, and dinners to give me time to study and write. We will share this degree as it belongs to them just as much as it belongs to me.

Thank you, my friends, who are also my family. Thank you for understanding that I wanted to be with you during many celebrations, events, and vacations, but had to stay behind to study and write. You kept me in your thoughts, prayers, and even through pictures of the fun I missed. I thank you for being with me through this journey and bringing me dinners and watching my dog when I needed a break to write.

I also want to thank the ladies in my life who have been my support system since I was a teenager. My aunt, Odessa, thank you for praying for me and giving me a hard time when I wanted to stop. You pushed me through some tough times, and I love you for it. My godmother, Judy, who continues to be my mom, I thank you. Thank you for stepping in the gap so many times. You have inspired and supported me from undergraduate school, and I still hear you in my times of struggle. Thank you for loving a son you did not give birth to but continue to love as if you did. Thank you!

Finally, I want to thank my mother, Margaret, who continues to inspire and motivate me from heaven. I am still working to make you proud of your youngest son. Your love and support continue to cradle my heart and my passion to keep learning and keep. I am working to making the world a little better, just as I said I would do. Thank you, I love and miss you deeply!

Thank you!

Kenneth D. Davis, Ed. D

NOTE TO THE READER:

Intentional Mentoring is one of those works that's close to my heart. I was mentored during several critical points in my life. My hope is that every child, young adult, and/or adult can learn, interact with and experience a mentor-mentee relationship. Mentors are special people and are not paid for their passion (*I call it God's work*). This book provides the steps, the thinking, the planning, and the research to the effectiveness of mentoring, and shares what I learned while organizing, implementing, and overseeing the Mentoring Project. It provides you (the reader) with invaluable information and a snapshot of what it can do for your organization, if followed. It made a difference for me, and my hopes are… it will do the same for you.

LIVING life has been a challenge yet I'm LEARNING that LAUGHING and LOVING are free, easy, and provides opportunities that I could have missed. I've grown up in poverty, disadvantaged communities, and have had obstacles to overcome. Haven't we all! Yet if it had not been for my career in education, I would not have experienced being MENTORED as I continued my education while LEADING others. I've spent 31 years in education working to encourage, inspire, became a teacher and after many promotions eventually becoming an area superintendent. In my growth and aspirations, I'm working on LIVING THE LEGACY I want to leave and providing a blueprint of what a successful career can look like. Intentional Mentoring is the LIVING LEGACY I choose to leave you, my community, and the world as I strive to make life better for all mankind one mentor-mentee relationship at a time. It is the path I was created to take.

Dr. Kenneth D. Davis

TABLE OF CONTENTS

INTRODUCTION

This book is more than just a guide for developing a successful mentoring program. It is also a CALL to ACTION for people to create, develop, sustain, and support mentoring programs within their organization, school system, corporation, church, community, etc. Everyone needs a mentor to become the best and most productive version of themselves during specific seasons of life. The statistics provided throughout this book are only the beginning of what can motivate and inspire people to become mentors or when seeking a mentor. The more I think about the reasons and my motivation behind the mentoring program I designed, the more I realize we need more mentoring programs, and this book is my contribution to guiding and assisting you in building a viable, sustainable, and successful mentoring program. It speaks to my over-arching goals in presenting this information to continue paving the road where every student, new employee, leader and/or human being has a mentor they can talk to and share ideas with while building a mutually beneficial mentor/mentee relationship.

According to the New Oxford American Dictionary, a mentor is an experienced and trusted advisor; an experienced person in a company, college, or school who trains and counsels new employees or students. In the realm of mentoring, the ability to work with an individual or group to support the improvement of their personal and professional growth and development is critical to the overall purpose of the program. Students and adults need mentors to better understand their pathway and gain knowledge and guidance as they grow personally and/or professionally. Mentors help mentees find their way along the winding road called life to see the areas in their life that need improvement. Mentoring stimulates and/or inspires the mentee to grow, create personal and professional boundaries, and introduce the mentee to a world outside of the confines of their community. Resulting in a 'ripple' effect, where mentees become mentors, supporting the statistic that says 89% of those who have been mentored will mentor others.

The pros supporting mentoring far outweigh the cons of mentoring. Some examples are:

- According to Guider 2020, 25% of employees who enrolled in a mentoring program had a salary-grade change, compared to only 5% of workers who did not take part, and corporate sponsored mentoring programs boosted minority representation at the management level from 9% to 24%.
- By preparing young people for college and careers, mentoring helps develop the future workplace talent pipeline. Lessening the potential loss of human potential because of the educational achievement gap. (*Mentoring: At the crossroads of education, business, and community*, www.mentoring.org/mentoring-impact/, 2015)

- More than half of the Ascending to Men (ATM) mentees met or exceeded the expected progress on the State of Texas Assessment of Academic Readiness (STAAR), the state's student testing program based on the Texas Essential Knowledge and Skills curriculum standards. The mentees made overall gains in reading and math on the STAAR 3-8 compared to their peers who were not in a mentoring program.

- Students who meet regularly with their mentors are 52% less likely than their peers to skip a day of school and 37% less likely to skip a class. (*Public/Private Ventures Study of Big Brother Big Sister*, www.mentoring.org/mentoring-impact/, Thurlow, Sinclair & Johnson, 2002)

- The Role of Risk Study says the strongest benefit from mentoring, and most consistent across risk groups, was a reduction in depressive symptoms — particularly noteworthy given that almost one in four youth reported worrisome levels of these symptoms at baseline. (*The Role of Risk*, www.mentoring.org/mentoring-impact/, 2013)

- Mentoring promotes positive social attitudes and relationships. Mentored youth trust their parents more and communicate better with them. (*The Role of Risk*, www.mentoring.org/mentoring-impact/, 2013)

Research and statistics support the necessity of having a mentoring program and action plan in organizations, companies, school systems, churches, etc. Regardless of the placement or location of the mentoring program, a viable mentoring program increases opportunities for all stakeholders. The key or secret ingredient in each program is in its development and programming, the identification of the ideal mentor that meets the specific needs, goals, and objectives of the overall program. In the same way businesses use marketing to attract their ideal customer, when developing a mentoring program, the planners must have their ideal mentor in mind to create a program that speaks to their strengths, experience, and knowledge base.

It will also speak to how the mentee will directly benefit from their leadership.

The mentee is not the only one who benefits from the mentor/mentee relationship. The mentor/mentee relationship and its corresponding programming have the potential for stimulating the passion and drive of the mentor while catapulting them on a pathway towards achieving their own personal and professional goals. In corporate America, mentors are six times more likely to be promoted while 89% of mentees believe their colleagues value their work, compared with 75% who do not have a mentor (Guider 2020 Statistical References). Almost anyone can mentor if they have their heart and mind in the right place and do not expect a return on their investment. The mentors value the developing relationship and their investment in the life of their mentee, and the mentees value the investment they have made in themselves and their exposure to unknown opportunities and possibilities. Research has proven there are benefits to having a mentoring program and mentor action plan (*Mentoring Statistics: The Research You Need To Know*, https://www.guider-ai.com/blog/mentoring-statistics-the-research-you-need-to-know, 02/03/2020, by Nicola Cronin).

The Intentional Mentoring 101 concept and construct is based upon the lessons learned and the success experienced while designing, establishing, and overseeing the Mentoring Project in the Houston Independent School district during the 2018-2019 school year for the Ascending to Men (ATM) Project for males from grades 3-12 and the Resilient Outstanding Sisters Exemplifying Success (ROSES) for females from grades 3-12 during the 2019-2020 school year. Although the initial programming began during the 2018-2019 school year, it continues to support students from elementary to postgraduate of high school. It is from this that I realized the economical, personal, and professional benefits of having a mentoring program not only within the school but also within the community, organizations and/or corporate America.

As you continue reading, you will find different instances where I share the statistical analysis and personal reflections and observations from the success we experienced and are still experiencing with the Mentoring Project. I truly believe that with a solid foundation you too can develop a successful mentoring program that will be beneficial to both the mentor and mentee while providing the mentee with invaluable information that has the power to help them make better choices and/or decisions in life, business and within their family.

Dr. Kenneth D. Davis

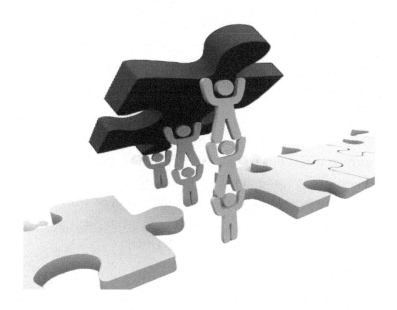

INTENTIONAL MENTORING
101

T he start of a mentoring program sets the stage for the development of a successful mentoring program that evolves to meet the varied needs of each class of mentees. When building a sustainable and effective mentoring program model, there are specific nuances that must be considered.

The most important consideration is the culture and environment in which the mentoring program will take place. Every business, school, and/or community has a specific culture and environment in which they conduct business. They have core values that are the foundation on which they are built and challenges they seek to overcome. All of which need to be considered when developing a mentoring program and identifying the mentees who will benefit from the program. Even in the mentoring program I designed, I had to look at the culture and environments of the schools involved in the program, in which the students (mentees) lived, and in which the mentors lived, worked and/or conducted business to tweak the overall program to meet the unique and identified needs as it relates to the program planning and the programming offered to both the mentors and mentees.

In my work in several school districts in Texas, I have created, developed, and implemented mentoring programs for boys and girls from elementary to high school. The program was focused on improving specific benchmarks by introducing mentors into the students' lives to provide guidance and model the desired behaviors in front of them consistently. The benchmarks I used were centered on the mentee's:

- academic achievement,
- emotional, mental, physical, and social wellbeing,
- culturally based obstacles.

The Mentoring Project was developed to have specific volunteer mentors who went through a rigorous training program before being matched with a mentee. The success or failure of any mentoring program is determined by the caliber and commitment of its mentors. Later in this book, we will talk about how to develop a successful mentoring program, the staff necessary to run the program, how to identify the program's stakeholders, and what your ideal mentor avatar looks like. By the time you reach the end of this book you will clearly understand how to develop your mentoring program and your ideal mentor. The programming will be structured to build a successful program with a clearly defined vision and guidelines.

Mentoring Programs are needed by every organization, business, school system, etc. need as they create an environment that builds, honors, and encourages servant leaders, not just workers. In the same way every business or organization is not the same, each mentoring program will be developed with the nuances specific to its own community and/or organizational structure. The basis of this book is to provide a step-by-step guide for building a successful mentoring program, and not to change the culture or the way a school, business or organization conducts business.

Mentoring programs are usually voluntary for both mentors and mentees; however, both must buy into the program to ensure its success. Although paid staff is not needed to carry out day-to-day functions, paid upper management staffing roles are needed to ensure fidelity and consistency with the programming. Even though the steps listed in the following chapters are not a final list, it should be considered as a suggested blueprint. It is suggested that various aspects of the culture of the school, business, or organization be incorporated to maintain their core values. The information and steps contained herein can save you planning time and offer a framework to build a successful mentoring program with a clearly defined structure, programming, and organization.

In this book, you will find the strategic and tactical considerations for systematically designing, developing, implementing, and overseeing your organization's mentoring program. I will also highlight the 6 pillars we used during mentoring sessions and share tools and various resources that were used during the Mentoring Project.

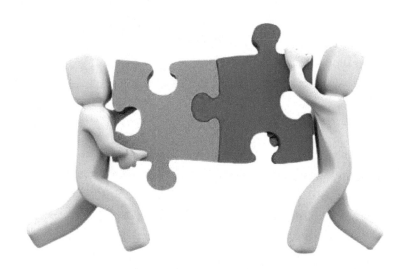

CHAPTER 1: FRAMEWORK

The framework is the most important aspect of any mentoring program, in the same way it is essential for the continued growth of an organization, school system and/or business and its employees and/or students. It provides the structure needed to ensure the goals and objectives are clearly defined and communicated to its stakeholders. The framework needs to be fluid to grow and expand to meet the needs of the mentees it serves and in how it recruits and trains the staff and mentors who implement and oversee the program. As the program continues to develop, the impact to the community in which it serves will be life changing.

Humans are designed to be in relationship with each other, and to learn peer-to-peer. Mentoring is one of the greatest vehicles any business, organization and/or school system can use to foster a learning experience that encourages building positive relationships that promote personal and professional growth. With the added benefit of positively impacting both the mentor and mentee's lives, which affects their family, community, and the world positively one mentor/mentee relationship at a time. Understanding the dynamic of a successful mentoring program and its expected outcomes begins with a framework that is designed in a way that empowers everyone involved to:

- show up,
- speak the same language, and
- understand what is expected of them.

According to the *7 ways to Structure Mentoring Program to Improve their Reach*, (www.trainingindustry.com, December 11, 2019, by Pritika Padhi) article, "...*mentoring... has existed as an informal learning method... to maximize the benefit of this natural human relationship... it is important to have a structure* (framework)." In the article, Pritika says that clarity around what the mentor/mentee relationship looks like is very important. The support staff, mentors and mentees need to know what is expected of them, the goals of the program, the structure of their mentoring sessions and the benefits of participating in the program. All of which are necessary ingredients for a successful mentoring program's framework.

Pritika also suggests that the mentoring experience be topical, explore different formats/models, allows for self-matching (giving participants a say in the matching process), build mentoring support systems (formal training programs for support staff and mentors with bite-sized refreshers and resources, develop a check-in system with mentors and mentees and provide a safe space for mentors and mentees to express their concerns and be heard), create a formal recognition program for mentors and mentees, and encourage the mentees to pay it forward (after the program, engage with mentees to have them endorse the mentoring program and/or become a mentor). Although these are great ideas, each mentoring program will design and develop its framework based upon the needs of the sponsoring organization and how they support their mentees.

Ascending To Men (ATM) Mentoring Project:

The Mentoring Project in the Houston Independent School District (HISD) focused on the individual and collective needs of the anticipated mentees. Focusing on their collective needs helped me to define and design a mentoring experience that ensures the goals and objectives of the program were met. The mentoring sessions included lessons on building relationships, building trust, interactions with the real-world community members who shared their skills and provided context to careers mentees wanted to learn about, and allowed the mentees to feel heard, seen and valued. Initially, 2,000 students signed up for the mentoring project and of them, 874 consistently attended the weekly ATM mentoring sessions during the 2018-2019 school year. Of those who consistently attended the mentoring programming, there was documented improvement in both their grades and attendance during the 2018-2019 school year. We implemented a mentoring component and several support activities and events, which included college visits, field trips, a Winter Ball, and Youth Summit. These activities created opportunities for mentors to bond with their mentees and opened the door to build trust relationships that led to additional opportunities for mentees to internalize the lessons learned from their mentors.

As with any program, not all students required a mentor and not all students selected to receive a mentor took part in the Mentoring Program. Those who actively participated in building a mentor/mentee relationship began displaying leadership qualities and achieving identified goals before the end of the 2018-2019 school year. In this chapter, we will focus on the framework necessary to build and sustain a successful mentoring program. We will begin with the framework, experiences, barriers, challenges, and successes we experienced with the HISD's Mentoring Project.

Four Models of Mentorship:

There are four basic models of mentorship: Traditional, Developmental, Group Based, and Peer Based which are proven effective models used in mentoring programs worldwide. Keep in mind that you need to know what is needed for the population you will serve. You may decide to pull from each model to develop your mentoring program if one model does not meet your specific needs. Below is a brief description of each mentorship model.

Traditional. The Traditional Mentoring Program model provides a one-on-one mentoring experience. This is where a mentee is matched with a mentor, and they partner to take part in building a strong, cohesive, and respectful mentoring relationship as specified in the construct of the overall mentoring program. Some formal one-on-one models may require participants to track their hours, performance goals, etc., to ensure both mentors and mentees are gaining value from the program through the mentor/mentee relationship. This type of mentoring is more focused on relationship building and individual skill building.

Developmental. The Developmental Model of mentoring is often used in a business setting. It typically pairs managers and upper management with employees as they progress in their careers over the course of a few years. This ensures the mentee is equipped to move into roles with more responsibility or that offers their desired advancement within their company or organization.

Group-Based. The Group-Based model is where a single mentor is matched with a cohort/group of mentees. In the group setting, mentees are encouraged to help each other stay on track and be accountable. The mentees have the added benefit of meeting with the mentor one-on-one when needed.

Peer-Based. In some Group-Based models, a mentor may not be needed as originally planned. The mentees meet in small groups to help one another by discussing the point of interests and sharing feedback. As they are learning about the new company, honing transferable skills and/or advancing in their career path, they mentor each other, eliminating the need for a mentor. They become accountability partners while helping each other achieve their professional and individual goals.

Ascending To Men Mentoring Project:

The school district's mentoring program was built on the traditional mentoring model; however, sometimes we used an aspect of the group mentoring model to help establish a safe place for the mentees to learn and grow into who they have the potential of becoming. By implementing aspects of the group mentoring model (e.g., college visits), we realized an unexpected benefit. The mentees became exposed to opportunities and possibilities that they otherwise would not have been exposed to or had access to. The shared experience during programming became a bedrock of our programming, even though our mentors used the traditional mentoring model when meeting with their mentees.

Now that you understand the four mentoring models, let's develop your program. The following is the system I used to develop the school district's mentoring program and that I encourage you to pull from when developing your mentoring program.

PROGRAM PRE-WORK

Step 1: Identify the system in which the program is needed.

As previously mentioned, every organization, company, church, business, etc., is different and their needs are different as well. These different needs should be reflected in the mentoring program's objectives. In this step, list the goals and objectives for your mentoring program. Consider if race, ethnicity, age, gender, socioeconomic status, religion, sexual orientation, culture, etc. will influence how you operate the mentoring program and/or mentor/mentee interactions. Make sure they are in line with your core values, vision, mission, and culture.

Dr. Kenneth D. Davis

Ask yourself the following questions:

1. What is the primary reason, rationale and/or goals for creating a mentoring program?
2. Why is the mentoring program needed?
3. Who are my stakeholders?
4. How will I use the four C's of successful mentoring programs (Clarity, Communication, Commitment, Confidence)?
5. Organizationally, what do I need to have developed and/or implemented to sustain my mentoring program?
6. Will there be an application and vetting process and/or referral process?
7. What will be the time period or what will be the length of the mentoring program?
8. Will the mentoring program be dependent on identified roles, annual time frames, milestones reached, etc.?
9. What issue or barrier does the mentoring program speak to and/or seek to resolve?
10. What are the expected outcomes of the program?
11. What resources are available for me to tap into?

Do your research.

To answer these and other questions, before creating the framework of any mentoring program, I suggest you do your research. Take the time to review the programming, outcomes, and structure of like mentoring programs. In almost anything in life, we know what we don't want before we know what we want. Research provides the necessary information to determine what will be best practices for your mentoring program. You can see what worked, what didn't work, what you do not want in your mentoring program and what is an essential ingredient in all mentoring programs.

By doing your research you can discover what will attract mentors and mentees to your program, identify who will most benefit from your mentoring program and what their specific needs are, what will motivate them to take part in a mentoring program, and determine the expectations of leadership and how to keep them engaged and supportive. Each program will look different based on the sponsoring organization and the needs of the mentees. Keep an open mind when doing your research. You may not use everything you learn, but you may learn from the mistakes made by other mentoring programs.

Stakeholders

A 'stakeholder' is a person with a vested interest in the operation, with different stakeholders having different angles of interest. These individuals or groups of people can hold the key to the success of your mentoring initiative, and identifying who the stakeholders are, and how best to influence them and get their support, is critical. (*Identifying and Influencing Key Stakeholders,* Jane Cranwell-Ward, Patricia Bossons and Sue Gover 2004, https://link.springer.com/chapter/10.1057%2F9780230509214 _8) The key stakeholders of any effective mentoring program should include the supporters, funders, program planners, mentor, mentee, program staff, and the institution. Keep in mind that the manner in which you communicate with each individual or group of stakeholders will need to be conveyed in a variety of different ways to ensure they receive the information relational to their role as a stakeholder and that meets the needs of the mentor, mentee, and community.

Four C's of Successful Mentoring Program

According to the *Clarity, Communication, Commitment – the key to successful mentoring programmes, (https://uk.intoo.com/cat-blog/the-key-to-successful-mentoring-programmes)*, a successful and effective mentoring program is based around three principles: Clarity, Communication and Commitment (I threw in the fourth one, Confidentiality, because it is a critical ingredient when developing the mentor/mentee relationship). Keep in mind that the mentors also used the four C's to help build a relationship between themselves and mentee.

- **Clarity of purpose** is essential when developing a mentoring program. It ensures they identify the right mentors, the correct measures are put in place, and they set the right expectations with both mentors and mentees in mind.

- **Communication** helps the planners determine how to share the goals and objectives, clarify roles, develop a marketing/advertising plan and/or speak to how the company, organization, school system, etc., is committed to and supports continuous learning as bedrocks of the mentoring program with stakeholders. It can also be the basis on which they create a communication plan that explains the individual benefits of having a mentoring program, how it will support their mission and vision and/or be used as a tool to attract their ideal mentor.

- **Commitment** is defined as the state or quality of being dedicated to a cause, activity, etc. As a part of the four C's, commitment refers to the dedication each entity has to the program. For any mentoring program to be truly effective or successful, there needs to be ongoing commitment by the stakeholders. Regardless of the role an individual may have within the construct of the mentoring program, they need to understand that they have agreed to be an active participant in the ongoing development, time investment, attentiveness, taking action, sharing ideas, etc. to ensure the successful longevity of the mentoring program.

- **<u>Confidentiality</u>** is defined as entrusted with private or restricted information. As it relates to a mentoring program, keeping the mentor's and mentee's personal information and/or their reason for participating in the program away from prying eyes is essential when showing their commitment to building trust with those who are overseeing the mentoring program. It isn't important for everyone to know who is involved in the mentoring program. However, the mentee and mentor can divulge that information if they choose to.

Clarity also speaks to the ability to build rapport and trust between the mentor and mentee, and how the mentor uses the art of questioning to gather needed information without putting the mentee "on guard" or offending them. It opens the door for the mentor to give critical feedback that helps the mentee grow and encourages them to step outside of their comfort zone to explore the world around them. Communication identifies the mentor's understanding and use of active listening skills (which speaks to why we have two ears and one mouth – to listen more than we speak), and how listening not only speaks to what is being said, but what is not being said, the mentee's body language, and instinctually knowing when the mentee isn't being honest and/or is holding back critical information. For mentors, their participation requires a commitment of their time, energy, skills, and abilities and/or developing a positive mentor/mentee relationship. For mentees, their participation ensures they are committed to building a positive relationship with their mentor, be open to learning from and being exposed to new experiences and gaining the most out of the mentor/mentee relationship. Overall, commitment refers to the mentors' and mentees' willingness to follow the guidelines/dictates of the mentoring program's framework.

KEY ELEMENTS TO CONSIDER DURING PLANNING

- How many participants will be enrolled in the program?
- The length of the program.
- What mentoring model will you use?
- Participant interactions/programming (how often will they take place and what will they look like. i.e., once a week, once a month, etc., in a meeting, in a group setting, individually, etc.).
- What type of reporting or progress tracking will be used [Four Levels of Evaluation: Reaction (participant feedback), Learning (ask questions to assess information learned), Behavioral (observe change in their behavior), Results (did the program produce expected outcomes/results)]?

MENTOR

a. **Identify your ideal mentor avatar.** When creating/developing a mentoring program, the program planners must determine who their ideal mentor is and what they look like, what are their assets, and what is their personality type. They must also have clearly defined attributes and know what they are looking for in a mentor. As well as know what personality type works best within their mentoring program model. Ask yourself, in my circle of influence, do I have anyone who immediately comes to mind when I think of who is a great mentor? Why? What characteristics do they have that make them a great mentor? What is their personality type? Are they adept at working with cultural differences? Do they respect and value diverse cultural backgrounds? Do they support diversity to enable and empower underrepresented racial/ethnic mentees? I would encourage you to brainstorm the answers to those questions and any additional characteristics that come to mind that would make someone an excellent mentor for your program. Keep in mind that not every successful business executive, business owner, teacher, and/or community leader are mentor material. On paper, they may seem perfect, however, do they professionally and personally check all the boxes of your predetermined criteria? Be careful not to make concessions to make someone fit the role when you know they don't. When designing your ideal mentor avatar, don't forget to consider the cultural differences and the diversity of the mentees, and any of their cultural or social boundaries.

THE ASCENDING TO MEN MENTORING PROJECT

In the School District's Mentoring Project, we had an available source of mentors. We identified members of our teaching staff as possible mentors and solicited mentors from the community, local businesses, etc. I must admit that not everyone who applied or volunteered to be a mentor was asked to be a mentor, and not everyone we asked agreed to be a mentor. Keep this in mind when selecting your mentors. It will keep you from being discouraged and frustrated. Remember, keep an open mind.

The Mentoring Project experienced some growing pains, as expected. During its inception, there were several recommendations and barriers that had to be addressed to prove the effectiveness of the Mentoring Project's design/framework. Initially, the school's leadership and teachers were key stakeholders where recommendations and barriers were identified. We discovered there was a need for greater school buy-in to incorporate the ATM Mentoring Project principles and strategies as part of the school's operational or wrap-around services. These principles and strategies focused on building relationships with other peers and adults. It became apparent there was a need to encourage the school personnel to display respectful behavior bridging an unexpected gap between staff, mentors, and mentees. It provided the basis for another bedrock of our program: mutual respect, patience, and support for everyone associated with the program. The inclusion of this bedrock helped us to address the ATM students' expressed opinions and the misunderstanding of students' experiences and perspectives by the adults they interacted with. Which presented us with the need to have dedicated spaces for mentoring sessions and group discussions. Previously, we talked about the 4th C, Confidentiality, this provided a safe place for our mentees to share their concerns and/or frustrations that became barriers to their learning.

During our planning sessions, we created the following overview, which was a goal for our mentoring program: *The Mentoring Project will seek to develop a 1:1 (traditional) mentoring relationship for males of color. The program will leverage community resources and partnerships to provide males of color with advocates (mentors) who will support them academically and socially and who will help them to aspire to attain a successful future. Students (mentees) taking part in the program will participate in a mentorship curriculum to help them address identified issues. They will attend workshops facilitated by adult males of color from various industries and attend entrepreneurship tours and college visits with the program culminating with a Mentor Summit at the end of the year.*

Step 2: Identify the role of the Program Director/Senior Program Manager.

Previously, we discussed the need for paid staff to have oversight of the program. The Program Director or Senior Program Manager is an essential ingredient in the planning, implementation, and oversight of the mentoring program. Responsibilities include:

- supervises the other paid and unpaid staff/team members,
- provides regular updates and/or progress reports to his/her leadership and/or stakeholders,
- responsible for keeping their finger on the pulse of the mentoring program and communicate the needs of the program, any changes made to programming, the organizational structure and dynamics, and the mission/vision of the program,
- develop the policies, procedures, and responsibilities of the Program Manager(s), Program Coordinator(s), mentors, and mentees,
- support the development and implementation of the program with fidelity,
- create the framework for the evaluation of the outcomes of the program, and
- help develop and support the funding tools needed to ensure the longevity and sustainability of the program.

Refer to the addendum for additional supportive documentation and guidance when hiring a Program Director or Senior Program Manager.

Step 3: Identify the role of the Supportive Team Members.

The supportive team members may comprise of program managers and/or program coordinators who are tasked with leading the development, implementation, and evaluation of the mentoring program. Their responsibilities include:

- actively take part in securing additional resources to support the sustainability and integrity of the program,
- implement the various components identified

- adjust the timeline of the program and build the infrastructure when faced with challenges and/or barriers.

A job summary and major duties and responsibilities of the Program Manager is provided in the Addendum for your review and/or use.

Step 4: Create a Training Plan.

Support Staff Training

The success of any program or project is founded on the training each role receives that actively participates in the program/project. According to *Why Is Training Necessary,* (https://www.dummies.com/business/human-resources/employee-engagement/why-is-training-necessary/, by Elaine Biech) article, "…*training plays an important role in developing a productive workforce and finely tuning processes to increase profits* [and receive desired outcomes]. *Training also helps people and organizations manage change.*" Below are four critical aspects of a coordinated comprehensive training approach, as provided by various sources:

1. **Structured Training and Development:** A structured training and development program ensures that employees have a consistent learning experience and background knowledge. Don't assume everyone is aware and can speak to the company/organization's mission and vision. Everyone needs to be aware of the core values, missions, vision, company/organization's policies. Include interval training sessions regularly that ensures all staff members are familiar and can regurgitate the program's mission and vision, and how it relates to the company/organization's mission/vision. (*The Importance of Training & Development in the Workplace,* https://smallbusiness.chron.com/importance-training-

development-workplace-10321.html, by Shelley Frost, Updated February 05, 2019)

2. **Untrained Workers are Inefficient**. More time (and therefore money) and effort are spent when employees aren't fully or properly trained to perform their tasks or to fulfill their responsibilities. It takes them longer to do the work, and they may need help from other employees to complete their tasks. (*Importance of Employee Training: 6 Reasons Why It Saves Money*, https://redshift.autodesk.com/importance-of-employee-training/, by Brian Benton, October 27, 2021) However, continued training will eliminate this problem.

3. **Exceeding Standards**: Training employees on industry-standard practices can give you a leg up on the competition. Small things often set your business apart from your competitors, so having employees that are knowledgeable and happy can improve interactions with mentors, mentees, other staff and/or stakeholders. (*Top 5 Reasons Why Employee Training Is Essential*, https://www.txtacc.com/blog/2018/04/top-5-reasons-why-employee-training-is-essential)

4. **It shows employees they are valued.** Implementing training programs in the workplace will help employees feel like the company is invested in them. By continuing to teach your employees new skills and abilities, they will not just become better workers, they will feel like more productive members of the organization. This will improve their sense of self and morale and their workplace capabilities. (*The Importance of Training Employees: 11 Benefits*, https://www.indeed.com/career-advice/career-development/importance-of-training, by Indeed Editorial Team, February 22, 2021)

The same 4 critical aspects should also be applied when designing and developing the training program for the mentors who will interact with the mentees your organization serves.

Dr. Kenneth D. Davis

MENTOR TRAINING PLAN:

A crucial aspect of every mentoring program is the point when the mentor understands their role in the mentee's life. However, it isn't something that can be taught. It must be experienced by the mentor and identified using the tips and tools covered during their mentor training. Creating a Mentor Training Plan that begins with the mentor's orientation and continues in the modules taught throughout their mentoring experience. The training ensures the mentor is equipped to handle the various situations they may encounter with their mentee and understand the responsibilities they have agreed to accept when becoming a mentor. A mentor is a powerful role in any organization, company and/or school system. Mentors have the ability and opportunity to teach and pass on valuable skills, knowledge, insight, and the importance of cultural awareness to a mentee. An effective Mentor Training Plan/Program must be established and implemented prior to the mentor having their initial contact with their mentee. This ensures the mentor is well equipped and prepared to have a successful mentoring experience.

This is where your ideal mentor avatar comes into play. Once your ideal mentor has been identified, you can create a mentor training program geared to bring out the best qualities and attributes of your program's mentors and identify their areas of weakness. It gives the planners the opportunity to meet each mentor where they are and bring them to the level, they need them to operate in when interacting with their mentee, all while providing them with the directives and resources specific to their program. This empowers the mentor to pass along their wealth of knowledge and experiences to the mentee in a way that inspires and empowers the mentee to act upon what they have learned.

What most mentoring programs, who do not train their mentors, cannot understand, is that an effective training program gives guidance to the mentors while mapping out the desired path the mentor is to take to experience a successful mentor/mentee relationship. There are two specific training methods planners of a mentoring program can choose from to use as their process or method when training their mentors:

1. **Self-Guided Courses**. The Self-Guided Course option is an efficient way to provide information and give the mentors the opportunity to learn on their own and at their own pace. However, there is no guarantee the material being covered is learned and/or understood by the mentor. Using this concept is a missed opportunity to ask questions of a facilitator and learn from others during the training.

2. **Live Training or Supplemental Workshops**. This option ensures mentors are familiar with the program's administrators and processes and provides an opportunity to clear up any misconceptions a mentor may have when learning and interpreting the training information.

The following are some suggested topics to cover during the mentor training program (*The Importance of training Your Mentors*, www.insala.com, June 24, 2019):

1. **Identifying the Mentoring Program Objective**. The mentoring program's goals and objectives should be shared during the mentor training and throughout the program. Remember, we learn through repetition.

2. **Explain the dynamics of a mentor/mentee relationship**. The best way to understand the dynamics of a mentor/mentee relationship is to recognize that the relationship between the mentor and mentee is personal. By including this as an aspect of the mentor training program, the mentor receives a clear idea about how to formulate a trusting and respectful relationship with their mentee, clearly identify their

expectations, develop trust, and effectively communicate with their mentee.

3. **Promote the benefits of being a mentor**. Share what mentors can expect to get out of their mentoring experience. It affords the mentor the opportunity to be more engaged and invested in their role as a mentor.

4. **Provide a role profile for both the mentor and mentee**. Role profiles offer clarity and guidance through the mentor/mentee relationship. Teach and remind mentors that the mentor/mentee relationship is always mentee driven and mentor guided.

5. **Define phases of the relationship**. Share with mentors the established timeline of check-ins, group activities, etc. It lets the mentor know what to expect and how to set the pace when building a mentor/mentee relationship that is built on trust and respect while honoring the mentoring program's timeline.

6. **Provide tips, ideas, and tools the mentor can use to build a trusting relationship**. Provide the mentor with tools, tips, ideas, and direction for their mentoring experience. This ensures the programming will be covered and goals will be set. It will also ensure the mentor understands and uses the programming as provided.

Some tools a mentor can be taught to use during their mentor/mentee experience are (*2 Tools for Success as A Mentor*, www.insala.com, March 6, 2019):

a.) **Using the SMART Goals Method**. Mentors can be taught how to set SMART (Specific, Measurable, Attainable, Realistic, Time-bound) goals as it relates to their mentor/mentee relationship and the identified strengths and weaknesses of the mentee that require improvement. It empowers the mentors to set mutually beneficial goals with their mentee that will benefit them during the mentoring program and throughout life.

b.) **Perform a Strength, Weakness, Opportunity, & Threat (SWOT) Analysis**. Teaching mentors how to go through a SWOT analysis with their mentee at the beginning of their relationship is an invaluable tool that can be utilized throughout their relationship to evaluate the mentee's growth and/or identify the achievements of their goals. The SWOT analysis identifies the mentees' strengths, weaknesses, opportunities, and threats. Keep in mind that a SWOT analysis is different for youth and adults. Be sure to use it to meet the needs of the mentees and as it relates to their age.

NOTE: The key importance of a SWOT analysis for youth is to help them achieve a clear picture of where they stand. It helps youth identify areas of improvement, set goals, identify what opportunities are ahead and recognize potential obstacles they may face that might hinder them from moving forward, achieving goals and/or experiencing the life they desire to live. More information on using SWOT Analysis as a tool in a mentoring program is provided in the Addendum.

7. **Highlight possible challenges the mentor may encounter with suggested solutions**. Let mentors know what they may face and give them workable solutions on how to handle the challenges if they occur. Have this portion of the training focused on preparing, equipping, and empowering the mentor to act in a manner that is conducive to the mission and vision of the mentoring program.

8. **Discuss how to transition the relationship once the life cycle of the mentoring experience has concluded**. Give various scenarios of what it looks like when ending the

mentor/mentee relationship on a positive note. By doing so, it leaves room for the mentor and mentee to change the aspect of their relationship to that of a friendship if it is desired.

Trained mentors can form positive and working relationships built on mutual trust and respect that help both the mentor and mentee develop lasting and mutually beneficial partnerships in the future. By requiring all mentors to complete the mentor trainings it ensures those charged with oversight of the program maintain quality control of their mentoring program, mentors, and mentees.

Step 5: Identify the PURPOSE of the program.

To ensure everyone understands the reason the mentoring program is created, can effectively communicate it to others and ensure all stakeholders are speaking the same language is why the mentoring program MUST have a clearly defined purpose statement, objective and/or overview. *"What is a purpose statement?"*

PURPOSE STATEMENT: A purpose statement is a declarative statement that summarizes the mentoring program's fundamental goals. It provides guidance and answers the questions "why" in "why are you creating a mentoring program?" According to *The Power of Purpose: 7 Elements of A Great Purpose Statement,* (www.forbes.com, by Afdhel Aziz, February 18, 2020) article, *"…having a clear and compelling purpose is… essential* [it] *seeks to attract talent, inspire its community…"* and allows your project/program to stand out in a sea of like programs. The article also says *"…a purpose can act as a North Star, a guiding light…* [that identifies] *…what they are all there to accomplish…"*

Keep in mind when writing/developing your purpose statement that it sets expectations, acts as a blueprint for the future, and helps guide all the decisions made for the program. There are three important reasons for developing a clear and concise purpose statement (*How to Develop Your Company's Purpose Statement*, www.wgu.edu, August 9, 2021):

1. Distinguishes your program from others. It defines what makes your program unique.
2. Helps meet goals. It sets a path for moving forward, which brings clarity when setting attainable goals.
3. Informs the Culture. When a mentoring program's purpose statement is clearly communicated, it allows all stakeholders to become connected and invested in the program and committed to supporting the goals of the program.

The following are seven aspects of a great purpose statement:

1. **Inspiring**. It should be memorable, aspirational, inspirational, and easy for everyone to learn and share it.
2. **Concise**. It should be as short and sweet as possible, yet memorable.
3. **Desired Outcome**. The role of the mentoring program and the overarching outcome it wishes to see in the world should be clearly identified. It should clearly state what it does for its stakeholders.
4. **Problem Solving**. What issue or community disparity are you seeking to provide a solution for? This should be easily identified in the purpose statement.
5. **Aspiring & Precise.** It needs to be clearly stated and not open to the reader's interpretation. It should be precise, but not limiting.
6. **Socially Responsible**. It should speak to or describe the social or environmental issue it seeks to solve.
7. **Evolving.** A great purpose statement is not stagnant, it develops as the program develops to continuously meet the needs of its participants, the context around its creation changes, and/or adaptable for any changes made to reframe the program and/or what it seeks to accomplish.

MENTORING PROJECT

When I was designing the 'Mentor Project' overview, I developed the model that was used when training mentors, getting student buy-in and getting the administration, teachers, and parents to see the value of the mentoring program, we were bringing to the school district. In it, I was able to answer the who, what, when, where, why, and how of the mentoring program:

Who: The Mentor Project will seek to develop 1:1 mentoring relationships with males of color?

What: The program will leverage community resources and partnerships to provide males of color with advocates who will support them academically, socially, and who will help them aspire towards a more advantageous future.

When: During the school year.

Where: In each identified school.

Why: To help students address the academic and social issues, seen as barriers, while providing them with the tools to help them visualize having and experiencing a successful future. (*In the Houston Independent School District, we discovered that African American and Hispanic males and females underperform academically in comparison to their peers in almost every category. We intimated that if we could improve the performance of this subgroup, we would be able to improve the overall performance of the district.*)

How: Students will participate in 1:1 mentoring sessions and workshops led by adult males of color from various industries within the community. We will leverage existing community programs and supports with the resources within the district by providing a network of mentors capable of supporting males and females of color culturally, socially, and academically.

Core Objectives:

- To build student self-reliance and resilience
- To build healthy attachments/relationships
- To improve positive connections to adults and peers in the school environment
- To enhance social, communication, relationship, and decision-making skills

Step 6: Outcomes

Identify the intended outcomes/accomplishments of the program and what the mentees will do when they complete the program. For this to be effective, the purpose/objectives for the mentoring program must be established. It provides the framework for the outcomes. Whereas the purpose answers the "why" question, the outcomes answer the "what" and "how." When determining the outcomes, it should be completed in two parts: action and content. The action speaks to the desired result or performance followed by a specific description of the program's content (Academic Programs and Planning, https://academicprograms.edu, adopted from California University, Bakersfield, PACT Outcomes Assessment Handbook, 1999). The following are some questions you can ask yourself when developing the outcomes for your mentoring program: What is the desired result of the program? What will be improved or changed? What will the participants say is the value of the program? How will it be accomplished?

Setting attainable outcomes is critical to the success of your mentoring program and in your efforts to measure them. When developing your outcomes (*Setting Better Outcomes* Blogpost, by Phanh Pam, www.asianefficiency.com/goals/setting-better-goals):

1. Structure your outcomes with a name, a why, a how and set defined and expected results.
2. Make your outcomes specific/concise where they are focused on one thing.
3. Record your outcomes and how they went. Do this even if you could not complete a task as an expected outcome. Record the who, what, and why a decision and an action were done.

MENTORING PROJECT:

The Mentoring Project was started on the premise from the data that showed a sub-group of students who struggled with attendance, behavior, school performance, and attitude were mainly male students of color, followed closely by female students of color. To increase the overall performance of the organization, a plan of action needed to be implemented with a supportive structure that would have a positive impact on the mentees. Thereby, creating an option for them to change their behavior as it relates to the areas previously mentioned. This identified group of students needed additional support, and there was not a program currently in place to meet them where they were, support them and challenge them to become better students and assets to their families, the school, and their community. Locations were then ranked from within the school system based upon those schools who presented the highest need to the lowest need for this proposed supportive community. The resources of human capital and finances determined how many locations could receive support from the program initially. If successful, this project would support students by equipping and empowering them to change their own lives and improve their overall performance. (*Research demonstrates that successful mentorship can lead to improved parental and peer relationships, increased positive decision making; thereby, decreasing negative behavioral interactions and consequences, decreased involvement with drugs, alcohol and gangs, improved confidence in completing schoolwork, and decreased rates of absenteeism.)*

While planning and overseeing the Mentoring Project, I discovered corporate America operates similarly. Regardless of the setting, mentors provide guidance, advice, feedback, and support to their mentee. A mentor serves as a role model, teacher, counselor, advisor, and/or advocate, depending on the mentee's specific goals and objectives. In the workplace, novice employees benefit from a mentor who can help guide them through the processes and procedures within the organization, and the role's specific duties and expectations. It is my belief that everyone should have a mentor when coming into a new or changing environment to grow, develop, and build towards a successful future.

Corporations are designed to meet their bottom line and make a profit; whereas schools are designed to develop a supportive environment where students can learn and thrive. They both are focused on the bottom line: meeting their goals and objectives. Schools want their students to graduate and move forward towards college, career and/or the military. Corporate institutions and/or organizations want their employees to grow and expand their professional growth opportunities. In all instances, by providing a mentoring program, it ensures the continuous growth and success of the company, organization and/or school system.

In the same way, the school's structure teaches and equips students with the tools necessary for them to graduate and move forward towards college, the military and/or a career; corporations are designed to create, equip, and empower a workforce that helps them achieve their mission and vision. Both seek to provide an environment that speaks to their growth and success, and by exposing students or employees to successful mentoring programs, it offers them a better chance of realizing their dreams and/or desired outcomes.

Let me quantify and qualify my previous statement, "...*everyone needs to experience the mentor/mentee relationship...*" According to Guider 2020 Statistical References, career development is crucial for individuals seeking to plan their career path. 25% of employees who enroll in a company sponsored mentoring program have experienced a salary grade change, compared to only 5% of workers who did not take part. Within the same framework, 89% of those with a mentor believed their work is valued, compared to the 75% who did not have a mentor. Also, 94% of employees said they would stay at a company longer if they were offered opportunities to learn and grow. Lastly, 89% of those who have been mentored mentor others, which is an unexpected and unanticipated benefit of any mentoring program. When mentees become mentors, the mentoring program comes full circle. In the mentoring programs where the mentee becomes the mentor, statistics show those mentors are enabled, equipped, and empowered to use the tools they developed as mentees to create an environment where positive change is encouraged, expected, and portrayed. Effecting positive change within themselves, the mentees, their communities, and the world.

EXPECT THE UNEXPECTED AND/OR UNINTENDED OUTCOMES.

Although you may design a successful mentoring program and experience the success you desire, there will always be evidence of unexpected and unintended outcomes. So, be on the lookout for them. Some will be positive, while others will cause you to return to the drawing board to ensure it is not an outcome in the future. This is one reason why your program needs to be fluid, allowing you to tweak it whenever and wherever necessary.

During the inception of the Mentoring Project, there were several individuals who worked against our efforts, making the process harder than it should have been. The School District's superintendent was in full support of the project. She gave me the leeway I needed to form, create, and develop the Mentoring Project to meet the specific needs of the student population it would serve. Individuals with hidden agendas quickly became hinderances to the project. Their words did not match their actions. They claimed to support the superintendent, but their undercover work was to ensure the mentoring project was unsuccessful. We experienced challenges with the funding necessary to kick off the project, and when implementing the various program phases designed to ensure the longevity of the project. As I am thinking about this, I remember when it came time to hire the program managers, things did not go as expected. The usual approval process directed me to the superintendent or their designee. After a few of these undercover roadblocks became apparent to the superintendent, she cut out the middleman and instructed me to submit all financial and staffing requests to him, first.

It was understandable, until it wasn't! We expected communication to get lost in a school system as large as the one I worked for. However, that was not the case. I realized some individuals wanted the attention and spotlight that seemed to accompany the mentoring project and conducted themselves in a manner that caused us to have to deal with unexpected challenges. What they did not count on was that we used the challenges to see how we could make the Mentoring Project better and expand it to support more students. Without intending to, their actions caused the Mentoring Project to be better and more structured than originally planned. Although I was a little skeptical, my excitement about the launch, how the Mentoring Project would be received by the mentors, mentees, school personnel and the community, won out.

I cannot say that all the unintended challenges affected the project negatively because they didn't. The Mentoring Project experienced some unexpected and unintended positives as well. Parents and mentees reported:

- improved parental and peer relationships,
- increased positive decision-making,
- decreased negative behavior interactions, and consequences,
- decreased involvement with drugs, alcohol and/or gangs,
- improved confidence in completing schoolwork, and
- decreased rates of absenteeism.

In the same way we experienced these positives, there were some students who chose not to benefit from the program and mentors. To decrease the instances of unexpected negative challenges, we created a process where both mentors and mentees gave feedback on how to improve the mentoring project model. The feedback we received helped us to expect unexpected and unintended challenges that influenced the Mentoring Project's outcomes and began having conversations to develop alternatives to redirect and/or refocus the project to reach as many mentors and mentees as possible.

In so doing, we could provide additional programming, create an even more supportive environment with access to social services as an extension of the program. They became additional services offered to the mentors/mentees taking part in the mentoring project. As a result, we could meet our mentors and/or mentees where they were, undergird them, and empower them to attain their goals while experiencing the successes they never knew were a possibility for them.

Previously, I mentioned I was hesitant about how the project would be received because of some of the hard decision I had to make. Decisions that were based upon limited resources. One such decision occurred when I had to rank the schools in the district from highest need (socioeconomic status, free/reduced lunch percentages, minority males, minority females, discipline counts) to the lowest need to determine which schools would immediately benefit from the additional support to the school's staff, students, and teachers. I must admit, the reception was more than I could have ever imagined. The students loved it, the principals wanted more, and the campuses improved in student attendance, school performance, challenges with student behavior, and a boost in the student's confidence. The changes were palpable and easily recognizable in the student's grades, their willingness to cooperate, show respect and sharing their hopes and dreams for the future. As more schools heard about the work being done with the Mentoring Project, requests came in asking when we would add more schools.

Although I wanted to put the Mentoring Project in every school, we still faced challenges in securing the funding necessary to hire additional support staff. Resulting from the School District dealing with funding shortages because of delayed state recapture payments, and the impact of Covid-19. To date, the Mentoring Project has not increased its staff or fiscal funding base since its inception. We do hope that will change as the positive impact and power of this project is realized district wide. It will also expose the need for a mentoring program in every organization, whether in a school district, non-profit, company or organization. As I have said before, I will say it again: *"Everyone needs a mentor."*

Even with the success the Mentoring Project experienced, we still were faced with challenges, funding restrictions and individuals with hidden agendas. We didn't allow any of that to stop our progress or cause us to shut down the Mentoring Project. It had the opposite affect! We became committed to the overall purpose of the Mentoring Project. We encourage any other mentoring program when faced with obstacles to remember their purpose and the impact their program can have. The power of your mentoring program is in the mentor/mentee relationship. A relationship that supports personal growth, builds healthy self-esteem, and builds trust for both the mentor and mentee. A relationship that has a ripple effect in the mentee's home, school, professional and personal life and/or their community. All of which affords them the opportunity to leave a legacy of positivity that potentially impacts every home community and/or organization. Which in turn begins building a better world for everyone to live in.

Step 7: Program Evaluation.

Determine how the program will be evaluated to measure the successes of the program. When determining the success or failure of any mentoring program, someone must conduct periodical evaluations to verify if the mentoring program is producing the expected outcomes. This must be an aspect of the planning process because it provides the planners with valuable information that can bring in more resources and/or add additional components to the program to help the program remain relevant. Evaluating the success or failure of your mentoring program involves two aspects: objectives and outcomes.

The process that has been suggested as an effective evaluation tool when identifying the program's stated objectives, define the Key Performance Indicators (KPIs), and what outcomes best speak to the success of your mentoring program. Knowing your objectives helps to identify what to measure and by identifying what you consider as success helps to interpret and use the data derived from your evaluation to improve upon your mentoring program and/or restructure the program to better meet the needs of the mentee population you are serving. There are several tools planners can use to conduct their evaluation. The following are the ones I consider as most effective and can be used at various intervals during the lifecycle of your mentoring program.

PROGRAM ADHERENCE. Program Adherence refers to a person or group understanding the purpose, goals, and expected outcomes of a program to know how to follow the program's guidelines and how to get the expected outcomes. When completing the program as designed, each participant (i.e., mentors and mentees) will show compliance with the program's guidelines, complete activities as instructed, and take part in outings as requested to ensure the program's success and the delivery of its expected outcomes.

Adherence to the structure and guidelines of the program means the objectives, guidelines curriculum, and activities are followed to the extent it ensures compliance is attained. Through its execution, it will identify if the program complies with the program's structure and guidelines, and allow you to address any issues identified, while developing alternatives whenever necessary to get the program moving forward and delivering the expected outcomes. The following are some steps to take to analyze a program's compliance with expected outcomes:

1. Determine if the initial program's goals and/or objectives are met.
2. Check periodically for noncompliance. (Are the lessons being taught, goals attained, or left unmet, etc.)

3. Identify any deficiencies in the program's performance, mentor activities, mentee progress, etc. (As it relates to the Program's SMART goals and SWOT outputs.)
4. Implement program interventions and/or program updates to correct inconsistencies and improve the mentoring program.
5. Consideration if the tools used to measure the program's adherence are correctly identifying opportunities for improvement and/or expansion.

PULSE CHECK. A pulse check happens when the program staff completes regular scheduled check-ins with mentors and mentees. It checks for consistency and checks for program adherence. Each pulse check should use the same questions:

MENTEE QUESTIONS:

1. Have you met with your mentor within the last week (determine how often you will conduct the post check)? Yes/No (Add a point system for each yes and each no answer)?
2. Are you completing programming/curriculum with your mentor?
3. Are you getting along with your mentor?
4. Are you attending the planned group activities and/or outings?

MENTOR QUESTIONS:

1. Are you getting along with your mentee?
2. Are you completing programming/curriculum with your mentee?

PROGRAM ADVOCACY. Program advocacy is the measurement of the impact on retention. It examines the retention rate of the mentors/mentees who participate in the program (the number who began versus the number who complete the program). From year to year, the program advocacy data can develop strategies to attract and keep interested mentors and mentees. This can include asking those who left the program to complete an evaluation/survey (similar to an exit interview). There can also be an evaluation/survey for those who choose not to participate in the program to complete. These evaluations/surveys can be incentivized to get the data needed. This is invaluable data/information when determining ways to improve and/or restructure the program to increase the retention rates for the program and/or mentors and mentees.

KEY PERFORMANCE INDICATORS (KPIs). KPIs refer to a set of quantifiable measurements used to gauge a mentoring program's overall performance. KPIs help determine the program's strategic and operational achievements. The following are KPIs that can be used to evaluate your mentoring program:

- the number of mentors/mentees who signed up for the program and began the program,
- retention rate,
- average attendance at meetings, outings and/or programming,
- successful mentor/mentee match ups beginning; how many mentor/mentees kept their initial mentor/mentees pairing, and
- behavior within the program, did the program experience expected outcomes, etc.

A program KPIs may determine:

1. **Satisfaction**: Measure engagement and communication frequency between mentor/mentee by analyzing the data derived from the number of meetups compared to the number of expected meetings and asking both the

mentor/mentee if they were/are satisfied with the program, their mentor/mentee match up, etc.

2. **Engagement**: Evaluates how effective a program is at achieving their objectives, goals, and expected outcomes. KPI's will vary from program to program depending upon several factors used, such as vision, mission, objectives, purpose, short/long-term goals, and/or expected outcomes. It's critical to prospectively determine what will be measured and how it will be measured. KPIs should serve as guideposts for staff, mentors and/or mentees when determining the success or failure of the program. KPIs can be used to derive the program's statistical data when the KPIs are engaged with the program's objectives. The following are some suggested steps to follow:

a) Define the program's definition of success.

b) Clearly identify the behaviors, actions, performance criteria that will lead to achieving the KPIs and hold staff, mentors and/or mentees accountable.

c) Ensure that stakeholders can communicate and understand clearly identified behaviors, actions, performance criteria, etc. Are they able to clearly identify and communicate with all staff members and whoever is the point of contact when help or support is needed?

KPIs will keep you mindful of ways to improve upon your program, its outcomes, and identify available resources. Some available evaluation tools you can use to evaluate a mentoring program are pre/post surveys, interviews, focus groups, goals sheet, etc. It is your responsibility to determine which tools will produce the information needed to measure the success or failure of your program.

Learning & Development: Did the mentor/mentee achieve the identified goals? Did they get what they expected out of the program? Was the program/curriculum effective in equipping the mentor and mentee to attain their individual and collective goals and improve their overall performance? When forming the questions as it relates to learning and development, consider developing questions that are tailored to match the mentor and mentee's level of comprehension. As they say, hindsight is 20/20. While creating and measuring the Mentoring Project's evaluation measures, another unexpected challenge presented itself. We saw where the challenges became a weapon used by those who did not support the program. Instead of getting angry and quitting, we brainstormed on how to overcome those challenges and strengthen the Mentoring Project. This is an opportunity for you to do the same and/or employ the 4 disciplines of execution.

PROGRAM IMPLEMENTATION

CREATE A MENTORING PROGRAM BOARD OF DIRECTORS (Advisory Council)

In any school system, corporation and/or organization, the board of directors is charged with governance, strategic planning/direction, and accountability. I believe that board members are the fiduciaries who steer the organization/company towards a sustainable future by adopting ethical, sound, and legal governance and fiscal management policies. A Board may also tap into available resources to advance the company or organization's mission. These requisite expectations are also true when creating a board that oversees your mentoring program.

Your board of directors should consist of recognized leaders from within your school system, corporation, the community, etc. These are the individuals who will help organize, oversee, and implement the various aspects of your mentoring program. Your mentoring program's governing board is the life's blood of your program. Which is why they should closely resemble and/or represent the community in which you will be serving. They should be diverse and from all walks of life. As well as culturally diverse to ensure the cultures of the mentees your program will serve are represented and/or have cultural awareness making them sensitive to the needs of the program's mentees.

Their input and commitment to the vision and mission of your mentoring program will help you stay on track. They will view the program from a higher level and have the vantage point to see things that those normally charged with the running of the program cannot see and make decisions that help the program evolve based on sound business judgment and not emotions.

The Mentoring Project did not have a board of directors. I reported directly to the Superintendent of the school system. Even though the Superintendent was completely supportive and was totally-engaged in the Mentoring Project, I believe having a board of directors would have helped negate some issues we experienced and allowed other key players within the school system and community to see the value of the mentoring program from within and/or support the program. Their buy-in and support may have opened more doors and/or made more resources available to the Mentoring Project.

GOVERNANCE

According to the Governance Institute of Australia, governance is defined as the framework that has the rules, relationships, systems, and processes within an organization which controls how decisions are made. This includes the paperwork, financial reports, program/process audits, contracts, staff/volunteer procedures, board records, and/or anything else that is written to ensure the purpose, objectives, mission, vision, and/or intent of the program is communicated effectively to members and stakeholders. The governance processes are usually built or approved by the board to direct the program and ensure the integrity of the program remains intact. Having proper governance in place creates a sound foundation on which to operate the program. (*What is Governance?*, Governance Institute of Australia, https://www.governanceinstitute.

com.au/resources/what-is-governance/; Governance Framework, https://en.wikipedia.org/wiki/Governance_framework;)

STRATEGIC DIRECTION

Strategic direction refers to the plans that need to be implemented for an organization or company to process towards its vision and fulfill its goals. It ensures stakeholders and management communicate the importance of their vision/mission and/or purpose of the mentoring program. As well as the importance of the mentor's role and their role in achieving the program's purpose. When forming your board, be sure to include individuals who have strong strategic experience in a broad range of industries, community organizations, etc. This affords you the opportunity to tap into resources that may not have otherwise been available to you and helps you plan for setbacks, the unexpected and the unintended.

ACCOUNTABILITY & OVERSIGHT

Accountability as an aspect of Board Governance is where the Board has a fundamental legal responsibility of ensuring the organization follows the laws, behaves ethically, and does not waste the resources trusted in its care. Accountability and oversight are directly tied to gaining the trust of the community and the stakeholders. There are tools available to you that ensure your Board meets the legal and ethical standards identified in the Boardsource.org Oversight and Accountability Recommended Governance Practices.

An effective, supportive, dialed in and committed board of directors is necessary to ensure the longevity of your mentoring program. The key is to keep your Board members engaged and included in all aspects of the mentoring program. It helps the communities in which they live, work and/or volunteer to see the great work you are doing and want to support your program as well.

For anyone to receive television coverage, social media exposure and/or secure impromptu interviews that inform the public of the impressive work you are doing is invaluable. In marketing, this is called unpaid advertising. It garners interest and attention to your program while creating a warm audience who may become the program's greatest advocates. This is a bonus from having a board of directors as the governing body for your mentoring program. You have resources to tap into from each director's sphere of influence, creating a win-win situation for your mentoring program. The key is to choose your board of directors wisely. Create an action plan on how you will recruit and retain board members, research the best practices, and develop a board that is an asset and not a hindrance to your mentoring program and its activities.

Your mentoring program's board of directors will be responsible for:

- developing and/or updating the mentoring programs' policies, procedures, staff roles, and responsibilities, and job descriptions
- oversee the development of the program's forms (enrollment, permission slips, photo permission forms, recruiting forms, program funding forms, and donation forms), and adopt them for use within the program and brand them with the mentoring program's logo and brand colors
- oversee the recruiting process when hiring staff, recruiting mentors, and screening mentees.

Splitting the board members into committees, is a better use of their strengths and existing networks – which is another benefit of a diverse board. The knowledge they bring can be the difference between facing a daunting task or completing the process with ease. Although you may have a lot of work completed, once your board is organized and has their inaugural meeting, all previously completed work must be presented to the board of directors for review to ensure it is legal and ethical for use within the confines of the mentoring program and are officially adopted and documented in the meeting minutes prior to implementation.

MENTORING PROJECT

I understand why some may forego developing a board of directors. However, it will still require you to have someone you report to that can see the bigger picture and has access to resources you can tap into. One of the unintended consequences that I experienced was that people who could have been invaluable assets to the Mentoring Project's failed to see themselves as key players. They saw the Mentoring Project as a one man show instead of a collaborative opportunity to support the students within the school system. There were even times when I felt they were working against my efforts because they misunderstood either my motives or the purpose of the program that created an adversarial relationship where everyone suffered, especially the mentees. We have had great success with the Mentoring Project. I sometimes wonder if we could have had greater success if those individuals would have seen themselves as assets and gave us access to their resources (e.g., financial, volunteers, advisors, etc.). Could we have put the Mentoring Project into more schools? Could we have developed a greater financial base? Could we have hired more staff? Could we have mentored more students? All these questions and more run through my head as I think about the Mentoring Project! I sometimes wonder if people truly realized the Mentoring Project was not about me, but about the mentors and mentees whose lives are positively impacted daily and the success they are and will experience throughout their lives. I was just the person who decided this was my way to give back and had the opportunity to use it as the subject of my dissertation. I am eternally grateful that my idea has had the success it has and is a program that can be modeled in any setting to help mentees see their value and positively impact the world, simply because someone exposed them to the possibilities and opportunities available to them. For the Mentoring Project and every other mentoring program, it takes a community of committed and supportive people who understand the assignment to ensure its success!

Regardless of which process you use, there are still developmental needs for your mentoring program framework that must be completed to create a viable mentoring program. Which includes (but not limited to):

1. **Develop the program's policies, procedures, roles, responsibilities, and job descriptions.**

   The vision, mission, values, and goals of the mentoring program must be developed to include the focus and intent for the board of directors/advisory council, advisors, mentees, mentors, and/or all other stakeholders. The vision and mission should include the goals that guide the one-to-one mentor/mentee relationship and the direction of the mentoring program. This may be an opportunity to create small committees with each committee responsible for the creation of each policy, procedure, role, and/or job description.

   During this process, it is better to keep it simple. Complicated policy driven challenges may hinder the development of the program. To avoid this issue, remain employee/student/mentee focused and mindful of your program's goals and objectives. Structure your program so that it enhances the experience for the mentees while supporting the mentors and program managers. Although the organizational structure may differ from program to program, the roles and responsibilities of a structured mentoring program should be similar.

   Director's Role/Responsibilities: The Director's role and responsibilities include the communication of the program's purpose and the need for the program to the system/organization and stakeholders within the larger community; development of the policies, procedures, and responsibilities of the Senior Program Manager, Program Managers, and students; securing the funding for the program from the system/organization for sustainability; supporting the development and implementation of the program with fidelity; and creating the framework for the evaluation of the program.

Senior Program Manager's Role/Responsibilities: The Senior Program Manager's role and responsibilities include:

- communicate the program purpose and the need for the program to stakeholders;
- seeking the additional funding for the program;
- supporting the development and implementation of the program;
- creating an Action Plan for the program;
- developing the Recruitment Plan for the program; and
- creating the Professional Development Plan for Program Managers and the Mentor Training for the mentors.

He/She is also responsible for the creation of the flowchart for the program and matches mentors with mentees.

2. **Develop and implement a recruiting process for staff and mentors, and a vetting process for mentees.**

The professional development and training for the staff will be critical in the program's alignment. The instructional content and leadership expectations are also developed within the program through specific training on:

- building relationships,
- leadership of mentors,
- the approved safety and security protocols,
- instructional lessons,
- the hierarchy of the system of communication,
- budgeting, and

- reporting results.

The recruiting process should provide the information in a hassle-free application process that is vetted through your Human Resource (HR) department or by an HR professional. All candidates must be vetted through a comprehensive process that includes criminal background and fingerprint checks to ensure the safety of the mentees participating in the program and the integrity of the program. This process should include prospectively defined criteria against which potential candidates are assessed. Specifically, those mentors and/or staff who have a criminal background by identifying any specific convictions that are allowable and why. Clearly define what your interview process will look like – recruiting, selecting, and onboarding. Identifying if a committee will interview each potential mentor and/or staff member? Develop the interview process and its levels. Clearly identify your approval process that moves candidates through the interview process to become a part of your mentoring program.

3. **Training.** Develop a separate training program/process for the mentors, mentees, and staff.

   a) If your mentoring program is using a Board of Directors or Advisory Council, each member will need training to understand Board Governance, strategic planning, accountability, and their role as it relates to your mentoring program.

   b) Staff will need training to manage the program, interact with superiors, continuously obtain stakeholders' buy-in with each new implementation of the program and/or when interacting with mentors, mentees, and the community.

   c) Mentors will need to take part in training to help them review curricula and facilitate conversations with the mentees to ensure the same message is being conveyed as designed for each lesson and/or mentor/mentee interaction.

d) Mentees will need to participate in training to understand the expectations of the program and to prepare them for their mentor (especially if they take part in the selection process).

Don't assume everyone will automatically understand their role as a part of the mentoring program and will act accordingly. Keep in mind that people don't know what they don't know! Share with all trainees – how the work is to be done and empower them to complete their roles, duties, and responsibilities ethically with authenticity and transparency.

Consider all aspects of the mentor/mentee interactions and determine any additional support they will need for facility access, leadership support and/or structure, program guidance and student interactions, etc. All these pieces should be included in the mentor training. Finally, the mentors are assigned to a mentee or small group of mentees and is supported by a program manager or assigned staff member responsible for 'shadowing' their mentor/mentee interactions for a few weeks until the novice mentor gets comfortable with their assigned duties and responsibilities. In the Addendum are sample mentor documents designed to support the framework of the mentor application and training process.

4. **Create clear goals and an evaluation process for the program, mentors, mentees, and staff.**

Goal setting needs to be a factor in determining the success and development of each mentor and mentee. Although the program is developed in alignment with project goals, individual goals are critical to the success of each participant, whether a mentor or mentee. Mentors may have goals related to increasing student enrollment and participation in the program, while mentees may have a goal of participation intending to foster a college-bound pathway. The program should be flexible enough to encompass the goals of all stakeholders.

5. **Create the mentoring program's curriculum/programming, supportive activities and outings that support the mentee's personal and professional development.**

Every program should have activities designed to engage the mentor and the mentee. These activities should have learning opportunities built in so that the mentee can practice what they've learned. Some activities may be as simple as talking about your thoughts from a picture or prompt that shows a child and parent holding hands walking along the beach. The mentees can discuss their experience that is similar, even if they have never done it. It exposes students to the idea of building relationships and expressing thoughts and feelings. The next activity would be for the mentees to visit a beach with their family or their program manager so that they are in a safe place of exploration. Activities should move from the abstract to the concrete, real world, so that mentees can practice and find success in the moment of the activities. These activities build bonding and learning opportunities that enhance their current and future relationships. It can change their life in ways that cannot be measured or even explained. Especially for those individuals who have been taught by the hard hits of life not to trust anyone.

6. **Develop all necessary forms for the program (enrollment, permission slips, photo permission form, recruiting forms, program funding/donation forms, etc.)**

Within the Mentoring Project, forms were created based on the need at each critical step and as identified. The application, training, and engagement with students should be a thorough process. A process that can be expanded as deemed necessary.

Dr. Kenneth D. Davis

7. **Develop the program's implementation action plan with the program's timeline/calendar and action owner**
   a. Spring/Summer Activities that need to be structured for a Fall Launch include the following processes:
      i. Create the Vision, Mission, Value, and Goals of the Mentoring Project.
         1. Mentoring Project's policies, programming, expectations, etc.
         2. Creating a budget for the Mentoring Project with Sustainability Plan
         3. Plan of Implementation for the Mentoring Project
      ii. Staffing for the Mentoring Project looking at the scope and size of the organization, district, school, church, etc.
         1. Director, Senior Manager, Program Managers
      iii. Program Criteria and supportive documentation for the mentor/mentee
         1. Attendance, academic performance, behavior, socioeconomic status,
      iv. Criteria for mentors: the program will need to support students
         1. Application, background check, and training process; in-person or virtual engagement with students
      v. Training for the Mentoring Project
         1. Master Schedule Adjustment to incorporate mentoring time with program manager and mentors
            a. Meet with principals, counselors for scheduling, and then assistant principals and finally teachers

b. Staff meeting during late summer early fall to introduce the Mentoring Project and the expectations for the mentees.

2. Share the student rosters that meet the criteria and adjusted student schedules as needed

vi. Fall Implementation of the Action Plan for the district and schools

vii. End of School Year Evaluation Tool to track and monitor program progress and performance

b. The Resilient Outstanding Sisters Exemplifying Success (ROSES) Project was designed along the same premise as the Ascending To Men (ATM) Project; however, it would be for the girls. The grade levels would be the same and be incorporated into the same schools as the ATM Project because of the criteria the school originally met for program acceptance. The ROSES Project mimics the ATM Project with all forms and programming, but it was designed for female mentors, mentees, program managers, and senior program managers all being female.

i. I came up with the program name by looking at my favorite flower (one of the few that I'm not allergic to) and created the mnemonic from there as a reflection of the female mentoring project, ROSES.

ii. ROSES provided the same support to females who meet the criteria for the mentoring program.

iii. The ATM program was developed first, knowing that it would take longer to get the programming and components in place to recruit the boys and sustainability of the program. The ROSES project would not be such a heavy lift, as predicted. There was also the concern that if the girls' project were developed first, boys would not be interested because of the potential assumption that the ATM program would be a copy of the ROSES. The mental shift was enough to persuade the development of the program and create the more challenging project (ATM) first.

c. The Mentoring Project encompasses both the ATM and ROSES Projects and supports culminating events, Winter Ball, college visits, and overall program gatherings.

    i. Some programming is gender specific regarding presentations, mentor assignments, some college visits, etc.

The activities in the program can be conducted in isolation, depending on the mentee's needs. For example, if a group of mentees is curious about learning to cook, the program manager may want to bring in a chef to talk to the mentees and share his/her story about becoming a chef and the joys of cooking. Other activities can be considered to incorporate all mentees from across the organization for everyone to gather and have a learning opportunity together, i.e., the Balls/Dance, college visits, etc.

8. Create the program's advertisement/marketing plan.

Every mentoring program's marketing plan will be different based upon who their target audience is, even though the techniques and/or tools may be universal. The key to a successful marketing program is to attract the mentoring program's ideal mentor and mentee or target audience. Creating content and timetable the distribution of the program's content is crucial to reaching your mentoring program's target audience. The following are some tips, tools, and techniques any mentoring program can employ to effectively market their program.

DEVELOP A MARKETING STRATEGY

This is where your program's vision, mission, goals, and programming will come into play. By already having developed each, the content and the story used to market the program can easily be written and communicated. Understanding the identified goals will help you remain focused and quickly identify where to interact with your target audience. It will also help you develop your marketing timeline as it relates to the mentoring program's timeline. Although the two may intersect or cross, they should not be the same. They should not overlap.

A. IDENTIFY YOUR TARGET AUDIENCE

For every mentoring program, the target audience encompasses two specific groups (and must be clearly identified and addressed): the ideal mentor and ideal mentee. By crafting your marketing message in a way that addresses the purpose of the mentoring program and its desired outcome, it will attract both simultaneously. The content or messaging used should be developed by sharing how your target audience will benefit (what will they get out of the experience) from actively taking part in your program. Most people desire to be part of something successful and you can capitalize on that basic need when creating your marketing message.

B. CRAFT YOUR MESSAGE

The key here is to remember, you have a very small window of time to catch the attention of your identified target audience. Keep your message simple, to the point, and easy for them to comprehend. One that will replay in their minds and hearts while compelling them to take action-participate in your mentoring program. The following are some tips you can use to craft your message:

- Tell the story. When telling the story, communicate the complete picture. Share the reason they want to take part, the level of commitment you are looking for, the benefits of participating and the call to action (what they need to do to participate)

- Determine the mediums you will use to reach and interact with your target audience.
- Decide who will be the face of the mentoring program and will deliver your message. The person needs to be completely dialed into what the vision and message are and convey it in a unique and compelling way.

When creating your marketing message, provide the information that makes your mentoring program stand out in the crowd. One that is unique, clear, and immediately catches the attention of your target audience. It should make them do a double take! One that compels them to learn more and act.

C. DEVELOP YOUR MARKETING PLAN'S TIMELINE

Once you have completed your research and developed your ideal mentor and mentee avatars (target audience), determine the best time to advertise, the best tools to use when advertising and the best platforms used to share your message where your target audience will hear it. All of those are necessary to ensure your message reaches your target audience. If you use social media to help spread your message, consider the block of time your target audience may be online. If using an email campaign, determine the best time period to send your email to ensure it does not get lost in their sea of emails.

Your timeline should begin 5-6 weeks prior to the launch of your mentoring program. This will create a buzz within the community where your target audience lives. It will also create excitement and anticipation. Some marketing plans use a stages approach. This is where you structure the timing of your marketing campaign to be the most effective. The following is a suggested stage-structured marketing campaign (*Best Practices for Marketing Your Mentoring Program*, www.insala.com, June 20, 2019):

1) Coming Soon: this builds the anticipation and excitement I mentioned earlier and should not be a one and done. It needs to be a strategic approach that has several interactions with your target audience. Map it out! Will it be video commercials, social media posts, informational events, scheduled announcements during community events, etc. Be intentional and purposeful when developing what this stage will look like and how it will impact the program while reaching your target audience.

2) Sign-up Now or Applications are now available: Continue sharing your message here. Consistency is the key! Just remember not to overdo it. Think about how you want to frame your message that causes your ideal mentors and mentees to respond as instructed. Think about this: the pictures on the wall in a person's living room may all be metal because it matches the room's décor. However, in the dining room or along the wall of the staircase, it may be different to match that décor. Your overall marketing message will not change, but how you frame and deliver it will change to catch the attention of individuals who are part of your target audience and compel them to act.

3) Do not Miss Out or Due Date for Application Submission is fast approaching: In every target audience you have two personalities that will respond during this stage: the procrastinator and the always late to the party person. By creating a marketing timeline that has a final push to give your program an opportunity to attract these personalities, you will find the diamonds in the rough. Why do you want them? They respond well under pressure. For some of

them they work best when under pressure. These personalities will ensure you stay engaged and will bring a level of excitement and commitment to your program's needs.

4) Program Success Stories: As you are overseeing your mentoring program, always be on the lookout for success stories you can incorporate into your marketing plan. This gives you an opportunity to brag on and share the great things happening within your program with potential funders, community supporters, potential mentors, and mentees, etc. As I stated previously, people have a great desire (need) to be part of something successful. This is your opportunity to shine a light on the great things happening in your mentoring program and in the lives of both the mentors and mentees.

D. POST LAUNCH MARKETING

Creating a post launch marketing plan helps you keep your mentoring program relevant. It is also an opportunity to share your program's success stories in real time. Remember, you have stakeholders and continued communication with them is critical to their continued support and the success of your program. This is also an opportunity for you to introduce, re-iterate, and/or repackage the topics discussed during mentor/mentee sessions in an email, newsletter, blog, video, or podcast. It will help keep everyone well informed and provide additional details on how to use the information and/or skills developed in the mentor's and mentee's everyday life. It is a known fact that we learn from repetition even when the message is packaged differently each time it's shared.

We have covered a lot of information in this chapter, and I challenge you to take it all under advisement when developing your marketing plan. Do your research and discover what works best for your mentoring program and when attracting your target audience (your ideal mentor and ideal mentee). How you do what you do makes your program unique. Build on that and watch your program experience the success you imagined. As Traub Manufacturing Company coined in 1927, *"often imitated, never duplicated,"* remember how you live the program's vision, mission, purpose, and/or goals make your mentoring program unique and stand out in the sea of mentoring programs to attract your target audience. As they say, it isn't always what you do, but how you do it that makes the difference.

9.   **Create the program's Kickoff and Sustainability Plan.**

Every community program and nonprofit organization must create a sustainability plan to ensure its ability to survive and thrive. Benjamin Franklin said, *"if you fail to plan, you are planning to fail."* This quote speaks to why your mentoring program needs to have a fully developed and executable sustainability plan. In all honesty, if you have completed the steps previously outlined in this book, you have already begun developing your sustainability plan.

Sustainability in the context of a mentoring program refers to the overall stability of the organization: its ability to weather temporary challenges, provide quality services in the present, make necessary changes because of social/economic challenges, and maintain a solid foundation for its future. Sustainability is impacted by all the key activities and functions of an organization and all major activities are affected by the ability of an organization to sustain itself (*The National Mentoring Center*). According to the *Mentoring Program Sustainability Plan Template*, *"The process of sustainability planning starts with reviewing the organization's resources and environment. Taking stock of the internal and external resources your organization has at its disposal."* It goes on to say, *"Sustainability requires a plan for services and practices that result in positive outcomes for children and youth and a plan for sharing the positive impact you create with your stakeholders in the community. Sustaining a mentoring program requires understanding of the systems in which it operates (e.g., schools, foster care, the juvenile justice system, churches, organizations, etc.), as well as the relevant policies and infrastructures that foster internal quality and stability… It is important to note that this process isn't necessarily linear and that the plan you develop is, and should be, a living document that requires frequent updates and adjustments to remain* [relevant and] *effective."*

CONCLUSION

The face of mentoring, its importance and its relevance have changed. In the past, only specific segments of society participated and benefited from mentoring. Today, organizations, companies and school corporations are developing mentoring programs that help them attain their stated goals and objectives. In today's world, mentoring has ceased to be an option to being a necessity. Each program enables, empowers, and equips individuals to become the leaders needed today and in the future. It offers those in leadership and in positions of power the opportunity to reach back and share what they have learned and experienced with others. They are teaching the importance of creating a culture of service-based leadership.

Mentoring is the opportunity for human-to-human and peer-to-peer interactions designed to provide guidance and leadership from mentor to mentee that's mutually beneficial. Although there are several mentoring programs active today, your program design will set your program apart from all the others. It is not about YOU creating or developing a viable mentoring program. It is your motives, vision, and mission that make up the foundation of your program. Understanding and being able to clearly communicate it to stakeholders, the impacted communities, and families of both the mentor and mentee ensures you will have an open source to secure qualified mentors and interested as well as invested mentees. As the organizer, the foundation you lay and the framework you structure for your mentoring program will determine if it stands and remains viable through the changes, challenges, and the tests of time.

If you ask anyone who has created/developed a mentoring program that has lasted five or more years they will tell you, that their program today is a different representation of their original blueprint. They will also tell you their originally drafted program was revised and/or re-evaluated to ensure its continued relevance and viability. With each new class of mentors and mentees, aspects of the program are tweaked to ensure the mentees received everything the program offers and more.

No two people are alike, even if they share common likes and/or dislikes. Something separates them to shine a light on their individual uniqueness. The same is true with and within your mentoring program. When we kicked off the Mentoring Project, I was excited and hopeful about our very promising future. I thought I knew everything I needed to know, and I was wrong! From development to implementation, I learned some things about myself and people that I am not sure I would have learned otherwise. It started off being about me, my vision, my hopes and dreams for the mentors and mentees to being about what is best for the program. I had to put my ego on the shelf and realize I am just the conduit being used to meet a need within the school district, the community, and in the lives of the mentors and mentees. I will not throw more statistics at you right now. What I am going to suggest you do before reading further is to step away. Take a minute to think about yourself as the mentor. What is your motivation? What tools do you need to mentor someone, and what level of commitment are you willing to offer to the program? Are you ALL in? Is this a resume builder? Are you unsure but willing to move forward and see how things will turn out? Sit in that space for a minute and truly determine who you will be when showing up as a mentor. This is truly an exercise in self-awareness, value, and commitment. Now, do the same thing with you being the mentee. Consider the uncertainty, instability, cultural biases, norms, and the systematic racism that impacts the lives of African Americans and people of color daily.

Think back to your childhood and feel those feelings of self-doubt, lack, and not being seen or heard. How can that knowledge and muscle memory assist you in creating a program for all people regardless of race, culture, financial status and/or class? A program that can be implemented in any setting: an organization, school, company, community, etc. Life teaches us to focus on self, be all you can be, and go after the brass ring.

A person committed to mentoring may say they have achieved a level of success and now I want to reach back within my community or company and share the vastness of my learned life lessons and wisdom with someone else to begin compiling their life toolbox to help:

- you recognize inconsistencies and correct them before implementation or as soon as possible,
- the mentor and mentee build a respectful and working relationship that sets the tone for every relationship going forward,
- reminds you daily that I am the master of my destiny. That also says if I want change, then I must be the change I want to see,
- empowers both the mentor and mentee to show up daily for themselves. As the scripture says, *"Charity begins at home and spreads abroad."* (1 Timothy 5:8)

Take the time to design your program before you determine the lessons covered as a part of your programming. Consider the environment in which your mentoring program will conduct business and implement programming. Will it be rolled out in a school district, as a community project, within the walls of a company or organization and/or to prepare individuals to become servant leaders within a church? From board governance to mentor/mentee training, each step along the journey is outlined in the pages of the chapter on framework. If you follow the map provided, when you are done you will have an exceptionally unique mentoring program designed to inform, inspire, encourage, enable, motivate, and empower both the mentor and mentee to become the best version of themselves while being a lifelong learner and adventurer. The challenges you face will seem pale compared to the joy you will experience upon completion of year one of your mentoring program. That joy will become the adrenaline you will use from now on to make the program better and able to meet the needs of the next class of mentors and mentees.

Each step you follow when building your mentoring program becomes the system in which you change the destiny for every mentor and mentee you serve. This investment in the upcoming generation of leaders, doctors, lawyers, politicians, celebrities, etc. ensures they are equipped, inspired, and empowered to show up prepared for the journey ahead. Isn't that what it is all about? Pouring into people while challenging them to fully and intentionally step into the opportunity to develop into the greatest version of themself.

Denzel Washington shared in an interview, "*I attended a local Boys & Girls Club with mentors who cared and gave me the confidence I needed to set higher goals than I might have... they gave me advice that became the bedrock of my thoughts on success. ...I learned a lot from my mentor, Billy Thomas, a Boys and Girls Club staff member. He impacted my career as an actor.*" I challenge you to be creative and own your process. It will change you and the lives of both the mentor and the mentee. Who knows the need your program will meet, the people it may impact and its ability to empower ordinary individuals to do extraordinary things? I encourage and implore you NOT to give up when things get difficult, but to tap into your reason why, embrace it and keep creating, building, and changing lives one mentor and mentee at a time. Malcolm X said, "*If not now, then when, if not me, then who?*" When experiencing doubt and/or the desire to give up or in, ask yourself the same question, "*If not now, then when, if not me, then who?*"

THE PILLARS:
INTRODUCTION

Throughout the history of humanity, it has become apparent that humans learn better when they participate in peer-to-peer learning opportunities. Mentoring is another aspect of peer-to-peer learning that presents the mentee with the modeling of behavior that leads to successful outcomes and firsthand experiences by identifying the skills and tools exemplified in leaders. Mentoring has become a universal opportunity to build a sense of self, improve personal and/or professional development, create a supportive learning environment, open avenues for exposure to opportunities and possibilities previously unknown and an emotional support system for both the mentor and the mentee. Which is why schools, corporations and organizations have created mentoring programs where leadership mentor's frontline and subordinate employees and/or youth. In schools, it has become even more effective when mentees are paired with educators who share their same ethnic and cultural beliefs.

In every instance, a mentee – whether students in an educational setting or adults in the workplace – benefits from the guidance mentors offer to better understand their pathway when navigating life and gaining knowledge. This is an essential ingredient in their development of their sense of self and when moving towards their purpose as they prepare to make decisions regarding their long-term personal and professional goals. The trust relationship that is built between the mentor and mentee empowers mentees to create a ripple effect, where they become a mentor to a new class of mentees. They take what they learned and experienced as a mentee and create a relationship with their mentee that introduces the mentee to a whole new world of opportunities and possibilities. The effectiveness of mentoring is why 89% of those who were mentored give back and become mentors. (10 Compelling Facts About National Mentoring Month, July 7, 2021, https://halo.com/10-compelling-facts-about-national-mentoring-month/)

The need for mentoring programs has not diminished over time, but because of its benefits for both the mentor and mentee, it is in demand even more. Every mentoring relationship should be viewed as mutually beneficial to both the mentor and mentee as they both seek to become a better version of themselves. Their consistent and positive interactions give them the opportunity to view the world and situations through the other person's eyes. As we cover the six pillars, we will share how each can have a positive impact on the lives of the mentor and mentee if used correctly to create a stable and sound foundation on which the mentoring relationship is built. Just like with everything else in life, a successful mentoring relationship will be designed with both the mentor's and mentee's individual and collective need to set boundaries, clarify expectations and participate in open communication in mind. This opens the door for the mentee and mentor to take part in and benefit from a rewarding and highly effective mentoring experience.

Why does anyone need a mentor? Many have proclaimed it is because they need the guidance to see beyond their limitations to discover the opportunities and/or possibilities available to them that have the potential of changing their future for the better. Others have said it is because it gives mentees insight into a realm of knowledge that was unknown to them (the mentee) that they can now envision themselves doing and/or living. Tomorrow is not promised to anyone and by having a mentor the mentee is provided with the needed information to develop a roadmap to living a better life than they believed was available to them. Especially in situations where the circumstances of their birth, and/or the cultural, racial, and/or economic disparities dictate their only options in life.

A mentor/mentee relationship has the potential of expanding the mentee's mindset from one full of the limitations to one that is limitless. What was not considered available to him/her becomes a myriad of possibilities that springs from the mentee's belief that nothing is impossible to him/her. For the mentor, they can introduce the unexpected and the previously thought impossible to their mentee and are afforded the unique opportunity to view the world through their mentee's eyes.

To truly see and experience the mentee's life in a way that empowers them to offer hope where only despair and hopelessness existed is the reality many mentors in youth-based programs experience. By preparing the mentee for what they may encounter and by training the mentor to introduce the human component into the following lessons, each mentor speaks to their mentee in a way that gives the mentee permission to take part in the conversations, learn the lessons, begin applying the lessons learned to their life, situation and/or circumstances and grow into who they now envision themselves as being. In turn, they become the successful, contributing members of society who have learned the importance of reaching back into their community, company, or organization and sharing what they learned as a mentee as they begin their new adventure of being a mentor. Building upon what has been given, taught, and shared with them during their mentee experience.

Life is about living, loving, learning, laughing, leading, and living your legacy. Each mentor and mentee live a life that represents what is left behind that says I lived, learned, shared, and touched lives to help them live their best life now. All while envisioning a world that offers opportunities and possibilities. The following pillars are structured to speak into both the heart, mind and lives of the mentor and mentee to realize their greatest potential as they envision a life founded on hope and hard work. A life that gives them the permission to take the blinders off and release the scales from their eyes to see what's there openly and honestly, while being vulnerable to the experience so they both walk away with a greater understanding of self and the knowledge that nothing is impossible to me. One that says if I can believe and conceive it (visualize it) and will do the work, it can become my reality.

This mutually beneficial relationship will equip both the mentor and mentee for the next season in their lives which reminds them never to forget who they once were. To forget is to return to what was to experience it again. However, growing and sharing their story of overcoming with others gives them permission to experience the hope that helps others continue growing, living, learning, loving, leading, and living their legacy as well!

"Anyone can follow a strategy as they read about it but remembering to stick with it in the real world is tough." –James Clear

Pillar 1: Lesson Structure

1. Intro: Getting to Know You Activity
   1. Intro to Mentoring Program
      a. Mission Statement
      b. Review of 6 Pillars
   2. Social and Emotional Learning
      a. Self-Awareness
      b. Self-Management
      c. Mentor/Mentee Interactions

Activities:

1. Have mentees write down and repeat the mentoring program's mission statement (Have mentors/mentees repeat it at the beginning of each session.) Find a way to make it relevant in the life of the mentor and mentee's relationship.

2. Review the six pillars by using culturally, socially and/or professionally relevant examples

   a. **Living**: Live every moment with a purpose (daily activities that are completed intentionally/purposefully, which are meant to help the mentee grow and have a better future).

   b. **Loving**: Love beyond words (Love is an action word and is to be used to help people reach their greatest potential). No act of love is too big or too small.

   c. **Learning**: is a conscious decision to change a person's perspective, viewpoint of self, and their view of the world around them.

Dr. Kenneth D. Davis

d. **Laughing**: finding amusement in a shared experience that connects humans in a profound way

e. **Leading**: is about serving others by utilizing their core values, personal and professional skills, and their genuine concern for people.

f. **Legacy**: is a living reflection of who you are, the legacy you desire to leave the world, and the greatest gift you give yourself, your family and the community.

To reiterate the point, have each mentor and mentee give an example of each pillar after learning what each one represents.

2. Social and Emotional Learning

a) Self-Awareness:
Self-Awareness is having a strong understanding of oneself. It includes understanding our thoughts, emotions, strengths, challenges, needs, and dreams for the future. Self-Awareness is important for children and youth because it sets the stage for success. It also means being aware of and/or able to reorganize how other people see you. (*Teaching Self Awareness, www.positiveaction.com*)

Suggested Lessons:

1. How to Identify Your Emotions

Help the mentee identify the difference between frustration and anger through (role play). Help the mentee recognize the link between their feelings, thoughts, and actions. This helps them learn how to address their feelings and respond to them appropriately. Encourage mentees to respond to life happening moments and/or situations instead of reacting to them. "*Responding is a spinoff from the word responsibility and is considerate and deliberate. Whereas reacting literally means to meet an action with another unplanned or thought-out action. It is immediate and rash.*" (A Simple Formula for Responding Not Reacting – The Growth Equation, https://thegrowtheq.com)

a. Reactions are instinctive.

b. Responses require thought and planning.

c. Discuss the Thought – Action – Feelings Circle. It is integral to our social and emotional curriculum, and in ensuring the mentee understands they can change the circumstances they experience based upon the choices/decisions they make. Dr. Phil said, "*when you choose the behavior, you also choose the consequence.*" It has the capability of depicting how the mentee's thoughts lead to their words and their words lead to actions which lead to their feelings, which starts the process all over again. Ultimately showing their character and their available destiny.

- Describe situations the mentee might find themselves in.

https://quizizz.com/admin/quiz/5e8a5491f5cd3a001ddb618e/thoughts-feelings-actions

- Discuss how those situations might make them feel, how and what they might think, and how they might act based on those thoughts and feelings. See yourself honestly.

Teaching your participants to look at themselves honestly can help them respond to compliments, feedback, and criticism openly and earnestly. This sense of self will enable them to see and acknowledge both the positive and negative aspects of their character.

a. Create Goals and Steps to Complete them.

Completing/Attaining their goals gives the mentee successes to celebrate, thereby fortifying their belief in themselves.

- Have mentees create and write down 3-5 life/personal goals and what steps they need to take to attain the goal. They will learn and understand that self-love and growth are positive activities that lead to healthy and happy people with a drive to achieve.

2. Recognize your Strengths and Weaknesses

Your mentee's ability to see themselves, acknowledge their shortcomings, and embrace their strengths is a great confidence booster. It reiterates that it is okay to admit they are wrong or don't understand something it sets them up for continued growth. Acknowledging aptitude also builds confidence.

- Use your strengths. Go through the process of helping your mentee to identify their strengths. The act of identifying things that your mentee is good at, reinforces a positive self-image. Keep in mind that working to improve their strengths builds self-confidence, setting them up for continued and future success.

b) Self-Management

This ties into some of what was discussed with self-awareness.

1. Self-Management is the ability to not only identify but regulate emotions, thoughts, and actions. It includes responsible decision-making that relates to the ability to make positive choices about the mentor's and mentee's behavior.

2. Behavior Monitoring

   Behavior Monitoring occurs when participants observe and record their behaviors, redirecting themselves whenever necessary to ensure the consequence is positive.

   a.) Self-Reinforcement is the act of rewarding oneself after completing the desired behavior or meeting a goal. Rewarding positive behavior increases the likelihood the mentee will repeat that behavior. (*Teaching Self-Management Skills: 5 Strategies to Create an Effective Plan,* www.positiveaction.net (blog))
   - According to Psychology Today, 85% of people who don't learn self-reinforcement have trouble in other areas, like self-esteem. Rewards can be anything that is healthy and motivates the mentee to act positively and/or reinforce positive behaviors.

c) Mentor/Mentee Interactions

1. Identify ways mentors and mentees can communicate. Establish the modes of communication the mentor and mentee will use.

2. In positive conflict, ideally, you can verbalize your needs and wants, and mutually work out beneficial compromises. The rule that all individuals agree to and operate in during the course of the mentor-mentee relationship defines

expectations (Rules of Engagement) that are important in your mentor-mentee relationship which creates a sense of safety. Rules of Engagement are the internal rules and procedures created to deal with unique circumstances and dedicate situations that require actions with significant consequences.

3. Mentors are encouraged to be innovative and creative when getting to know each other. The mentor should find ways to connect with their mentee to help build a trusting and respectful relationship. It is important they learn about each other. Especially those things that show their uniqueness.

4. Be reliable, consistent, and positive. Be present at each scheduled meet up in both mind and body. Pay attention to the mentee and their accomplishments and failures. Share constructive criticism and praise whenever necessary. Remember to always build the mentee up and allow them to recognize the good they have done and their wrongdoing and seek to change any negative behavior. (*Ten tips for a Successful Mentor-Mentee Relationship*, www.amtamassage.org)

LIVING

CHAPTER 2:
PILLAR: LIVING

I was listening to a daily meditation that said, *"Every problem is a gift! Without problems, we would not grow!"* That immediately made me think about mentoring. Why? Because mentoring is an answer to a societal, community, cultural and/or economic problem. It speaks to the lack that is represented in our world, and by implementing a viable mentoring program, the organizers can offer both hope and an answer to each participant's life's question.

Humanity is designed to be in relationship with and to interact with each other. To interact, live and/or experience life as a community and not alone. In this pillar, both the mentor and mentee will learn the importance of living and not merely existing. While implementing and overseeing the Mentoring Project, I witnessed firsthand how the mentor-mentee relationship gave the mentee permission to live and see life beyond the limitations that initially restricted their belief system, value their view of the world and recognize what was available to them.

The mentee was not only able to visualize a different future for themselves, but to begin speaking out loud the life they desire. Sometimes, they saw themselves as doctors, lawyers and/or educators instead of only athletes who uses sports to save them from a dying community and/or culture. Mentees will learn from their mentor that *"Your life is a physical manifestation of what is going on in your mind's eye"* – Unknown. Instead of dying in the streets of the community they were born or raised in, the mentee now can see the opportunities and possibilities available to them. In corporate America, the low-level employee could go from hating their job and struggling to barely put food on the table and barely pay their bills to preparing a roadmap for their future that equips and prepares them to follow their dreams or do something that makes their job exciting and beneficial. All while affording them the opportunity to make a salary conducive to their skills and abilities.

I know you are saying how can I have that component in my mentoring program. You begin with identifying the various limiting beliefs the mentees you will serve carry in their hearts and minds through group discussions, surveys and/or activities/lessons designed to get them to open up and share. Which showcases the need for you to train your mentors how to be culturally sensitive and understand how to recognize their biases to ensure they do not negatively impact the mentor-mentee relationship. Train your mentors on the components of open communication and encourage him/her to have open and informative dialogue with their mentee to derive the information they need while the mentee feels safe sharing with the certainty they will be seen or heard.

In most cases, life looks significantly different in the mentor's life than that of the mentee! The differences may be seen in how they live their lives, culturally, economically, racially, etc. Statistically a Caucasian living in the same house design in a predominantly white/Caucasian community property value is 37% higher than one in a predominantly black or community of color. This difference affects the amount of property taxes collected and money available to fund schools and other social services. Thereby, negatively impacting black communities and those of color ensuring there's a distinct difference in the resources and opportunities available to them.

Although these differences and disparities are a part of life, if both, the mentor, and mentee are committed to building a strong and respectful mentoring relationship, they together can work through any biases that may be present in both of their lives and viewpoints on life. In 2020 – 2021, there were protests, rallies, and speeches to bring the necessary people to the table to begin the conversations that can impact the lives and lifestyles of many people culturally, racially, and economically. It is in these settings that plans can be established to make conditions better and that promise to bring *some* equity to the equation that has been in place and is a part of the fabric of America.

The mindset of each of these individuals must change to ensure the conversations become a plan that is implemented. I share that to say the same thing needs to occur during the development of your mentoring program and in designing the lessons that will be the tool you used to effect change and offer hope to both the mentor and mentee who participates in your program. By having the conversations with a cross section of the community you want to impact, you will have the information necessary to impact their lives.

This Living Pillar humanizes and puts a face to all races, their lifestyles, and the conditions in which ALL people live. This pillar should help participants become more aware of the racial, economic, and cultural disparities people endure daily. Enabling them to determine the best way to offer hope and introduce opportunities and possibilities that may not have been previously considered by the mentee.

According to Sunshine Parenting, there are "*5 Ways to Teach Kids to Live Life Well*," (www.Sunshine-Parenting.com):

1. ***Unplug for a while each day.*** Whereas the article talked about unplugging from social media. I challenge you to take that a step further. Create activities and/or experiences where the mentee can unplug from their communities, daily limitations, homelife, etc. Provide them with time to experience something different and debrief. During your debriefing time, ask questions to understand how the experience or activity impacted the mentee. This will help to widen their knowledge base while exposing the mentee to experiences and activities they never saw themselves doing or participating in.

2. ***Interact with Others.*** This step encourages the mentees to maintain, nurture and build relationships. The mentee is to make it a priority to regularly communicate with friends, family and/or loved ones. As well as participate in activities that will encourage them to build new relationships. According to *"Health Benefits of Social Interactions"* (www.mercycare.org), *"spending quality time with friends, loved ones and/or others can lighten their mood and disposition* (better mental health), *lower the risk of dementia* (encourage good brain health), *promote a sense of safety, belonging and security and/or provides you with resources to share confidences."*

Let's take this a step forward and teach the mentee how to make new connections, how to handle themselves when meeting new people, and/or how to build relationships that will equip them with the tools, connections and/or relationships to rise out of their current situations that are steppingstones that have the potential of becoming lifelong friends.

Corporate America is moving away from the boardroom to closing business deals during dinner or when out having fun. With that in mind, teaching mentors and mentees how to conduct themselves and the proper dining etiquette during a business dinner may help relieve some of the nervousness and give them more confidence to secure the job or close the deal. By ensuring they have the skills that are needed when going after business ownership or corporate jobs is imperative, especially when those skills aren't used in their daily life and activities in their current community. Mentoring can expose the mentee to what is possible based upon what they aspire to be or do. Create an opportunity to use what they have learned. The experience can be life changing.

3. ***Take Care of You*** (your mind, body, and soul). Today, more people are sitting and are isolated from working remotely while completing their daily duties on a computer or for students in the physical or virtual classroom. The maintenance of your physical health is just as important as maintaining your mental health. Create an atmosphere where it is safe for the mentee and mentor to move through exercises, dance, etc. Something that will get them up and moving around. Find out what kind of dance your mentees are interested in and have someone to come in and teach them a routine. Then create an opportunity for them to perform it. This builds confidence, self-esteem, and encourages them to try new things. Even for those who have 2 left feet, help them find their spot in the production and/or planning. Whatever you decide, be sure to be up and moving together. This will not only improve their health but release those much-needed endorphins to overcome obstacles they encounter in life.

4. ***Learn to manage your time and priorities***. As I mentioned previously, time is our most valuable asset, or commodity. Learning how to use it will help with eliminating anxiety and feelings of being overwhelmed. I challenge you to have exercises and/or activities that teach organizational and time management skills. As a part of the exercise or activity, teach the importance of taking breaks while studying and/or working. It gives the brain time to refresh. This is also a time to get up and move around to kick off those endorphins to help you remain focused and on task.

This may also be a time to introduce meditation and/or visualization. Our thoughts form the life we lead and as such we need to show the mentee, the importance of visualizing themselves living the life they want, doing the job or having the career they want and/or running their business. The mind is the core engine that manifests the story each person tells themself. Through visualization, the person can change the narrative based upon the new information they have and visualize themselves being successful while living their best life. Teach them how to create their individual life and stay on track to manifest what they visualized into their reality.

5. ***Figure out what you like***. Seldomly do people have time to figure out what they want or like. We can more readily tell what we do not want rather than to state what we want. In school and on the job, we are told what to do and if we want this or that what we need or should be doing. Following this process does not teach anyone how to identify those things they believe will bring them happiness and/or ignite the drive to live their best life now. Look for different scenarios, activities, or experiences to help the mentee discover what he/she is passionate about. Give them an opportunity to experience the various hobbies to determine which one they are good at or interested in. This will help them live "...*thriving, vibrant, happy lives.*" And helps them flourish in the moment, and everyday thereafter.

Give yourself permission to think outside of societal lines and norms. Introduce mentees to the beauty within their community and outside of their communities. If you find graffiti that inspires and that has brought their community together, even if it was because of tragedy. Take them on a field trip to a small art studio or museum that showcases art from today's up and coming artists. If possible, have the artist visit the mentees to share their story and their art. Give them an opportunity to see that everyone's story matters and how they tell it indicates where their passion lies.

This can spark conversations that divulge the mental and emotional story the mentee tells him/herself to give the mentor further insight into how to reach, communicate, and inspire their mentee. The greatest life lessons are taught and learned outside of the classroom. Once again, give yourself permission to be creative to show both the mentor and mentee the importance of living a life that empowers and enables them to show up in their own life!

Dr. Kenneth D. Davis

LOVING

CHAPTER 3:
PILLAR: LOVING

Merriam's Dictionary defines love as a strong affection for another arising out of kinship or personal ties; attention based on affection and tenderness; affection based on admiration, benevolence, or common interest. As we understand love, we must first begin with the most important aspect of love: self-love, before moving to loving entities outside of ourselves. According to *"Self-Love and What it Means,"* (www.bbrfoundation.org, February 12, 2020), self-love is a state of appreciation for oneself that grows from actions that support our physical, psychological, and spiritual growth. Self-love means having a high regard for your own well-being and happiness (above that of others). Self-love means taking care of your own needs and not sacrificing your happiness and/or wellbeing to please others. Knowing your value and worth is what self-love is all about. Self-love means not settling for less than you deserve.

In the *"A Seven Step Prescription for Self-love"* article (www.psychologytoday.com, by Deborah Khoshaba, PsyD., 3/27/2012), there are seven steps to cultivate self-love, however, we will focus on only five of them:

1. ***Become Mindful.*** Take a minute and take the pulse of your self-love. Be mindful of who you believe yourself to be and act on this knowledge rather than focusing more on what others want for you. This connects with the mentee's lesson on living (discovering what he/she is passionate about) while learning how to make themself the most important person in their life. It is easier for him/her to discover their passions when they become mindful of who they are and are respecting and loving of themselves.

2. ***Acknowledge what you need rather than what you want.*** When a person learns to practice self-love, they can turn away from things that don't serve them, even if it looks and feel good or are emotionally gratifying. The person can focus on those things that are needed "...*to stay strong, centered, and moving forward in their life...*" By staying focused on what you need, you turn away from automatic behavior patterns that get you into trouble, stuck in the past, connected to things designed to destroy you and/or encourages self-destructive behaviors/actions.

3. ***Set Boundaries to Protect Yourself.*** In the article it states that a person who practices setting personal and professional boundaries will set limits on activities that deplete or harm them physically, emotionally, professionally, and spiritually or that poorly expressed who he/she is publicly and/or privately. It will help them correctly select and bring the right people into their life, especially those who are invited in to be a part of their inner circle. Having and building solid self-love enables and empowers him/her to remove those individuals who find pleasure in his/her pain and loss rather than

their success and happiness even if the person is a family member. Learning how to love from a distance will give him/her the space they need to focus on themself and their needs.

4. ***FORGIVE***. It seems like one of the hardest things to do in life is to forgive oneself for those things they have done or taken part in that have not serviced them and/or improved their view of themself. As humans, we seem to punish ourselves instead of accepting responsibility and forgiving ourselves. When practicing self-love, he/she must accept their humanness and their propensity to mess up every now and then. Learning to offer themself some forgiveness for not being perfect but cognizant of who they are. Remember there are no failures if he/she has learned and grown from their mistakes; they are only lessons learned.

5. ***Live Intentionally and Purposefully***. Live your life with purpose, and intentionally. While discovering your purpose, live a meaningful and healthy life. The decisions and choices you make will support this intention and help you see yourself in a positive light. It will help you learn how to love yourself even more when you see yourself accomplishing your goals and building a better life for yourself.

Helping both the mentor and mentee understand and begin practicing self-love will help them envision the life they want because now they see themselves as being worthy of having it. This is where setting personal goals, mapping them out, and celebrating their attainment is essential to their continued growth and development. Because it speaks to the love, they display or show themselves daily. When they learn the importance of loving themselves, it impacts how they talk to themselves and the mental dialogue they have with themselves. I once heard that "*...when you speak, I AM the unconscious mind says, 'you are so!'*" (*The I Am Principe*, by Charles Ogada, Published 2011) and moves behind the scenes to make what you have spoken to manifest itself in your reality. One important aspect of learning how to love ourselves empowers us to become kinder to ourselves and begin to speak about the future we desire in love and lovingly.

As the person learns how to love themselves, they can love and respect others in a manner that enables them to accept them where they are without it having a negative impact on them. The greatest gift one human can give another is love. As we take a deeper dive into loving as it relates to the relationships we nurture through love and respect, it is important that our personal definition represents the love we experienced early in life. The love that was shown within the family and village/community that helped to raise you or the lack thereof. However, it isn't the same, but it is the foundation on which we build self-love and the guiding love and respect that is developed in the mentor-mentee relationship and is being nurtured. The greatest gift a human can give another is LOVE.

As we take a deeper dive into loving as it relates to relationships, we nurture through love and respect. It is important that our personal definition is impacted by the love we experienced early in life. The love that was shown within the family and village/community that helped raise you or the lack thereof. This pillar rebuilds or renovates the foundation on which self-love, guiding love and respect are built as the mentor/mentee relationship is being nurtured.

GUIDING LOVE

Guiding love offers guidance from a mentor to the mentee and from mentee to mentor in the sharing of different aspects of their life, sharing their likes and dislikes, skills, abilities and/or areas of expertise and/or knowledge that exposes the mentee to opportunities and possibilities they otherwise would not have known is available to him/her. For the mentor, it gives him/her insight into how to best communicate and interact with their mentee. As well as giving the mentor the opportunity to realize the influences, hinderances and/or mindset of their mentee.

This type of love is founded on respect and a genuine desire for both parties to grow and succeed in life. The guiding-love shown from a mentor to a mentee opens them up to recognizes the need in their life to build a structured relationship through which the mentee benefits from receiving advice, wisdom, and instruction from a seasoned, caring, and engaging individual (mentor). All while gaining the awareness, respect and care when building the mentor-mentee relationship and interacting with people.

While researching guiding-love I discovered it is an aspect of agape love, an aspect of the five love languages kept showing up, and integral when building and nurturing any kind of relationship. Yes, even the guiding-love we have been discussing. The following is how it would be conceptualized in the mentor-mentee relationship: words of affirmation, quality time, acts of service, receiving gifts, and physical contact.

Scott Aoki says, "*I believe the love languages have a place in all human relationships and should play an active role in how we communicate as mentors and mentees.*" He also states, "*…the connection between a mentor and mentee can be a multifaceted mix of other personal and professional interactions… therefore it follows its own rules regarding personal interactions and open communication.*"

1. **WORDS OF AFFIRMATION**
   Words of affirmation include celebratory compliments that are shared after the mentor and/or mentee has accomplished an achievement or goal. It also includes moments when encouragement is needed, and/or when using a salutation and/or sharing one's opinion.

2. **QUALITY TIME**
   One of the most valuable assets a person has is time. Spending quality time when building the mentor/mentee relationship is paramount. What makes it quality time? When both the mentor and mentee attempt to make the time productive. It helps build confidence individually and collectively. Sometimes a kind or encouraging word said during a scheduled or impromptu interaction can be the difference between life and death.

3. **ACTS OF SERVICE**

   Throughout the mentoring relationship, there will be opportunities where the mentor may expose the mentee or vice versa to something that inspires, empowers and/or enables them to see life differently. It is found when they take part in community service projects and/or does something unexpected yet encouraging that builds another person's self-esteem. Keep in mind, acts of service within the mentoring relationship builds trust and respect. The act of service can be something small yet impactful or big, and thoughtful. Whichever it is, it speaks of the reverence and respect being developed between the mentor and mentee, and others.

4. **PHYSICAL TOUCH**

   This type of love language can be seen as too much for some; however, it is necessary even when building a supportive and respectful mentoring relationship. I am talking about something kind and innocent: a pat on the back, high-five, handshake, encouraging smile and/or eye contact during a conversation. These all can offer a level of communication between two people that encourages them to be and do better.

5. **RECEIVING GIFTS**

   At first glance, most people would say this love language is inappropriate in a mentoring program. I challenge that thought! Merriam-Webster's dictionary defines a gift or present as an item given to someone without the expectation of payment or anything in return. Giving the gift of knowledge, understanding, acceptance, skills, tools, examples to right living, and/or being seen are invaluable to the person receiving it. It isn't about the gift itself or the person giving it, as much as it is about the recipient (mentee) receiving it, opening it, and using it. Under this guise, giving gifts from mentor to mentee is not only necessary but required to ensure the mentee receives the pertinent information that fosters their mentor-mentee relationship, and equips the mentee with the information, tools, and/or skills to make wise choices and/or decisions in their life during the various stages of their growth and/or development personally and professionally.

The interpretation and use of these five love languages ensures both the mentor and mentee are benefiting from the mentoring relationship. It helps to shape their lives by going forward while encouraging them to show the best version of themselves each day. Love is an essential ingredient in human development and is essential when developing/building a mentoring relationship.

Dr. Kenneth D. Davis

CHAPTER 4:
PILLAR: LEARNING

Merriam-Webster dictionary defines learning as the acquisition of knowledge or skills through experience, study, or by being taught. In psychology, learning is defined as the relatively permanent change in behavior because of an experience. I sat in this space writing and rewriting this pillar concerned that the information being disseminated will be relevant, usable, and inspiring. So, I went back to the drawing board to determine why I chose education as a career. Like many others, I chose a career in education to help mold the minds and lives of the next generation. To help them navigate their educational career with the support, opportunities, and information that does more than just have students rotely memorize the information and regurgitated on a test, term paper, and/or during a class discussion. I wanted the lessons I taught to be seen as the living and exciting aspects of life, development, and growth they truly are. If I am being truthful, that is part of my motivation that energized and empowered me to begin the Mentoring Project. Take a minute and truly consider why you are considering starting a mentoring program and what you hope the mentor and mentee will take away from the experience. Initially, I was going to inundate you with the statistical data that proves the cultural, economic, and financial disparities that are woven into the fabric of America. Instead, I thought about the benefits of this pillar, as a level in the foundation both the mentor and mentee are building and securing, will be the place in which they spring forth to live the life of their choosing. So many times, people are judged by their last poor choice, bad act, circumstance surrounding their birth, and/or the communities they live in. I purposefully left out their race because that is a horse of a different color and is something that cannot be changed or taught. Everyone must come into the realization of self that is spoken about in the pillar on LIVING.

LEARNING is a choice, a conscious decision that is intentionally acted upon. It isn't something that happens by accident or unwillingly. Learning, if done correctly and received intentionally, has the power to change the person's perspective, viewpoint of themselves and their view of the world around them. It also influences how they allow the world to impact them and how they impact the world around them. I mentioned this before and find it relevant here as well. Doctor Phil said, "...*you cannot choose the behavior without also choosing the circumstance.*" That is also true in education. You cannot choose to be present and participate in the learning as it takes place and not receive the information shared to impact your life in some way, shape, or form. Nor can you walk away from the responsibility you now have to what you have learned. Which shines a light on what Maya Angelou said, "...*when you know better, do better.*" I know you are wondering why I ventured away from the style and playbook of the other pillars. The truth of the matter is this is one of the most important pillars the mentor will share with and teach to the mentee. The mentor must allow him/herself to learn the pillars on LIVING and LOVING to ensure they present the lesson on LEARNING in a way that encourages, empowers, and enables the mentee to accept responsibility for the information they receive and the courage to activate it in their life. In a way that gives them permission to envision a life outside of the confines of their community, home, and/or societal limitations.

Let's revisit the definition of learning. The key components of the definition are (1) acquisition, (2) knowledge, (3) skills, and (4) experience. Follow me here because I am going somewhere.

1. **Acquisition** is defined as an asset or object bought or obtained; the learning or developing of a skill, habit, or quality.
2. **Knowledge** is the facts, information, and skills gained by a person through experience or education; and awareness or familiarity gained by experience of a fact or situation.
3. **Skill** is the ability to do something well or with expertise, the ability to use one's knowledge effectively and readily.
4. **An Experience** is the process of doing and seeing things and of having things happen to you; an encounter, event, or occurrence.

Each of the words defined above are components of learning and are relative only to the individual who is experiencing the episode of learning that is occurring at that moment. Learning does not happen without each aspect that is previously mentioned happening simultaneously. All while empowering and enabling the learner to show up and take part in their own life to activate, cultivate, and give themselves permission to use the information in the season of life, it is most needed and effective.

LEARNING only happens when we see the value in acquiring or getting the information for internal or external use. Sometimes the information is only valuable to you because of your own personal values and the accomplishments you desire for your life. The value is determined based upon how the information can be used and how the learner will use it to change their perspectives, attitude, and altitude. I was watching a movie and there was a scene where the character was holding on for dear life because they did not know how far down the ground was beneath their feet. Another character came along to help them and didn't stop quick enough and ended up falling into the limitless and smoke covered bottom. Their landing resounded with a loud thud and when they stood up, their nose was at the same level as the other characters' waist. Once the character realized the floor was closer than they initially thought, they released what they were holding onto and dropped to the floor. The lack of information left character #1 uncertain and afraid to act or even move. However, once the character had the information they initially lacked, they received it and acted upon it. In that moment, character #1 had the freedom to make a decision that changed their perspective and made the decision that was the right one for them at that moment.

According to *4 Types of Learning Styles*, there are four learning styles: visual, auditory, reading and writing, and kinesthetic.

1. **Visual Learners** are better able to retain information when it is presented to them in a graphic depiction.
2. **Auditory Learners** prefer listening to information that is being presented vocally.
3. **Reading and Writing Learners** focus on the written word, reading and writing, and other text-heavy resources.
4. **Kinesthetic Learners** are hands-on thrive when engaging all their senses during coursework and/or learning opportunities.

For the mentee to benefit and find value in this pillar, the mentor must identify their unique learning style and present the information in a manner that catches the mentee's attention. Do not assume your mentee learns in the same way you do. Ask! Pay attention to him/her and see how he/she responds to the information. It will give you the insight you need to determine their learning style.

In mentoring, LEARNING is the component or the result that happens from each mentor-mentee interaction. Do not leave these experiences to chance. Plan them out with your mentee's style of learning and personal interests in mind. For the purposes of this book, LEARNING comprises the various ways information can be shared and/or introduced to the mentee during group sessions and/or individual mentor-mentee interactions. I have found that using open discussion after a lesson or an opportunity to experience the information learned in real time is more effective than just listening. For example, if the lesson is being taught on life skills, the mentor can offer real-life scenarios where the mentee applies the information, he/she has learned. This will provide the mentee with a reference point that helps them process and remember the information. Another example is if the lesson is about discipline and organization. The mentor can take their mentee to a ballet or interpretive dance program, and afterwards have a question-and-answer session with the dancers. During the session, the mentor and mentee can ask questions about what they did to reach their current level of success and/or how they've organized their lives to become successful dancers. The same scenario can be used with any profession. Once they finish the question-and-answer session, ask the mentees what they learned and to give an example of how they can incorporate the learned life lessons into their everyday life!

As mentioned before, learning is an experience and it presents itself differently based upon who is sharing or teaching the information, and who receives, interprets, and uses the information. Not to mention, how they decide to activate or use the information. The mentor may look at the information being shared as common-sense information, while the mentee is receiving new information that expands their awareness and their view of themselves, their community, and even the world. Which affords the mentor a rare yet rewarding opportunity to experience the occurrence through the wonderment and excitement as the mentee experiences it. It changes them both in that moment. The mentor develops a new point of reference that teaches him/her how to view, process, and/or share information going forward. The mentor realizes another aspect of who they are and how they can affect change in the world, one mentee at a time. The mentee receives the information and sees themselves in a larger picture or on a world stage. Whereas previously, they could not see themselves outside of the confines of their community and/or their cultural and/or economic limitations. They have the chance to envision a life that is limitless. Regardless of the setting, the opportunity to learn, grow, and evolve helps both the mentor and the mentee to develop and experience life differently going forward. During the mentor-mentee interactions, they both develop the role each will play in the other person's life, and in what their mentoring relationship needs to look like for them to continue growing forward. What most people cannot recognize or realize is that every experience and/or information received changes who each of them are especially when the impact of the experience/information has left an indelible mark on their heart and/or mind. A fact of life that cannot be disputed in any way is that while the mentor and mentee have breath in their body, they will be in a constant state of learning.

GUIDANCE

Throughout the history of mankind, it has become apparent that humans learn better when they take part in peer-to-peer learning opportunities. Mentoring is another aspect of peer-to-peer learning that presents the mentee with the modeling of behavior that leads or guides them to experiencing successful outcomes and first-hand experiences with identifying the skills and tools exemplified in leaders. Mentoring has become a universal opportunity to build a sense of self, improve personal and/or professional development, create a supportive learning environment, open avenues for exposure to opportunities and possibilities previously unknown to them, and an emotional support system for both the mentor and mentee during critical moments in each of their lives. Which is why schools, corporations, and organizations have created mentoring programs where leadership mentor's frontline and subordinate employees, teachers and/or community leaders mentor students/youth, and youth centers and/or youth organizations create programming where mentoring occurs in group settings. In schools, it has become even more effective when mentees are paired with educators who share their same ethnic and cultural beliefs. In corporations and/or organizations, it has become even more effective when mentees are paired with executive level personnel or community leaders who have attained the level of success they desire, but don't have access to.

In every instance, mentees, whether students in an educational setting, adults/youth in a community setting, or adults in the workplace, benefit from the guidance mentoring offers to better understand their pathway when navigating life, and when gaining knowledge. This is an essential ingredient in their development of their sense of self and when moving towards their purpose, they plan their long-term personal and/or professional goals. The trust relationship that is built between the mentor and mentee empowers the mentee to create a ripple effect, where they become a mentor to those coming up behind him/her. They take what they have learned and experienced as a mentee to create a relationship with a mentee that opens the mentee up to a whole new world of opportunities and possibilities.

Alan Bruce said, "*Even learning includes strong elements of guidance... these elements of guidance are to enable the mentee to reflect, consider options, and in the end make choices based on the information... Guidance can point out the consequences of choices made by the mentee...*" All of which are necessary for the mentee to grow and mature while developing the confidence that the choices/decisions they face may be the right one for them to make. While actively considering if it is the right choice/decision for him/her to make during this time in their life. This is the case regardless if the mentee is a youth or an employee in a Fortune 500 company. Learning involves the introduction and retention of information that opens his/her eyes to see a world that is more accessible to them and has the potential of opening doors they may have never known were available to them. Doors that offer him/her entrance, access and/or the lenses to see a world outside of the confines of the one they have become comfortable and content living within.

According to *The Master's Voice: Learning Through Mentoring,* "*Mentoring plays a valuable role in imparting skills, attitudes, and experience-based lessons to develop relationships of trust and interactive communication in a paradigm of shared goals. It is a neutral space... that plays a vital role in developing the critical judgement, analytical skills and decision-making skills necessary for continued growth and development throughout the various phases of life."* As the mentees have new experiences and take in more information, he/she understands and recognizes the choices they make today have the power to open or lock doors to the future currently available to him/her.

In every instance in my life, I have found anything worth having is worth working for, being committed to, and organizing my life to make it a reality. There is no greater feeling in the world than attaining your goals and respecting the hard work you put into it. That feeling of satisfaction can only be felt/experienced. Attempting to express those feelings in words does not do it justice! Which shines a light on the need for mentoring programs in schools, corporations and/or organizations and the benefits enjoyed by all stakeholders.

CHAPTER 5:
PILLAR: LAUGHING

Throughout life, many have been told not to take themselves too seriously. To enjoy life and to laugh more. In the previous chapters, the mentee has learned invaluable lessons, grown into who they are meant to be in this season of their life, learned the importance of giving themselves the gift of love and how to share it with others, and they have learned that their future is bright with opportunities and possibilities. All of which is necessary! Now it is time to learn how to LAUGH! Ella Wheeler Wilcox wrote, *"Laugh, and the world laughs with you; weep, and you weep alone."* In her musings, it became clear she implied that cheerful people draw cheerful people to them. She encourages people to keep their sense of humor! In this chapter, the mentee will build upon what they have learned and LAUGH!

The Importance of Laughter/Laughing

Wow, considering how to present this chapter on laughter, I came across the following *"laughter is the language of the soul,"* - Pablo Neruda. It sets the tone and direction I will use to describe the different uses for laughter and its healing properties. All of which speak to its necessity in our lives. Robert Provine says, *"...laughter is specifically a social structure, something that connects humans with one another in a profound way."* In his study, he found people are 30% more likely to laugh in a social setting that warrants it than when alone with a dash of humor inducing media. This supports his previous statement that humans are more likely to laugh with friends than when experiencing some comedic event alone.

There are many ways in which people resort to laughter: contagious laughter, nervous laughter, and canned laughter. If you think about it, 90% of our laughter has nothing to do with responding to the joke someone told, but for various other reasons. The following are four different types of laughter and the reasons why we may use them.

Contagious laughter: Think about the last time you were with friends or at a family gathering and someone tells a joke. A joke that isn't funny at all, but the person telling the joke laughs to the point of tears. Their laughter causes others to laugh and then you find yourself laughing. Laughing more because everyone else is laughing and not because the joke was funny and supports the belief that humans have laughed detectors. This belief is based on providing an explanation why people automatically respond to laughter with laughter.

Nervous laughter: Nervous laughter is used to protect a person's dignity and/or to maintain control of a situation. However, a small giggle or laugh can easily turn into uncontrollable laughter without warning. Nervous laughter is usually a person's subconscious attempt to reduce stress in order to calm down, but in most cases, it does the complete opposite. It usually heightens the uncomfortableness of the situation.

CANNED LAUGHTER: Canned laughter is genuine laughter that is taken completely out of context and place. Canned laughter is usually used to influence or cause an audience to find humor in the comedic material being shared or in response to it. This type of laughter is designed with contagious laughter in mind and was introduced in television in the 1950s.

CRUEL LAUGHTER: Cruel laughter is laughter that is used at another person's expense. It is considered as being cruel and insensitive. Most people who participate in cruel laughter did not initially set out to do so. For example, if someone falls and hurts himself/herself, and an onlooker laughs. Other witnesses look at him/her, thinking their laughter is inappropriate. The person laughing realizes its inappropriateness and tries to stop laughing, and sometimes they are successful but not always. However, at other times, they force themselves to leave because they cannot stop laughing. Their laughter isn't because they aren't concerned with the other individual's wellbeing, it is because something in the action of falling caused them to laugh.

LAUGHTER'S HEALING CAPABILITIES

Nothing releases endorphins from your brain, reduces the level of stress in your body, and strengthens the immune system than laughing. It is proven that laughter therapy, also known as humor therapy, can reduce negativity, emotional stress, and physical discomfort.

1. **Laughter is a natural painkiller**: Laughing produces hormones (happy brain chemicals) that act as a natural painkiller (reducing anxiety, easing chronic pain, and makes a person feel happy).
2. **Strengthens your heart.** Laughing is a cardio activity for the heart because it speeds up a person's heart rate.
3. **Wards off disease**: Laughing is a form of protection for your body. The more you laugh and approach life positively, the fewer chronic diseases you will develop.

4. **Tones your abs**: The action of laughing causes the muscles in your abdomen to contract (or flex) and relax (like when doing Ab crunches).
5. **Boosts immunity**: Laughing activates your body's T-cells (are immune system cells) to help ward off germs and illness.
6. **Decreases blood pressure**: Laughter decreases and maintains healthy blood pressure levels and lowers the risk of a heart attack and stroke.
7. **Banishes stress**: A few moments of laughter will reduce the level of stress hormones (i.e., cortisol) coursing around your abdomen area.
8. **Helps those suffering from depression**: Laughing can improve one's overall outlook on life; and eases emotional and physical discomfort and pain significantly.

COMBAT STRESS

1. **Stimulates many organs:** Laughing enhances your intake of oxygen rich air, stimulates your heart, lungs, and muscles, and increases the endorphins released by your brain.
2. **Activate your stress response**: Laughing cools down your stress release and increases your heart rate and decreases your blood pressure, leaving you feeling peaceful and relaxed.
3. **Soothes tension:** Laughing stimulates circulation and aids in muscle relaxation to release some of the physical symptoms of stress.

In every instance where there's laughter, it begins with a SMILE! Smiling activates tiny molecules in your brain that fends off stress and releases dopamine, endorphins and serotonin that lowers your anxiety while increasing feelings of happiness.

CHAPTER 6:
PILLAR: LEADING

Before anyone can become a leader of many, they must first become a leader of one: SELF. The core values the mentee has learned while on this journey are invaluable and transferable. However, to become an effective leader, the mentee must develop or enhance their leadership skills. Leadership is about serving others and isn't self-serving. As we step into the LEADERSHIP pillar, I challenge you not to lose sight of the self-work you have already done. That work should begin revealing the mentee's life plan and the journey he/she is to take. Some people are natural born leaders while others are taught to be leaders. Regardless which category the mentee falls into, to be an effective leader he/she must be concerned with people and their ability to learn the core values, systems, and processes that are the nuts and bolts of the company or organization in which they work. The expectations, skills and tools needed to secure a successful education; and their personal values, insight, and willingness to serve others are all the framework of an effective leader.

This pillar on LEADING begins first with the mentor before the mentee enters the picture. The mentor MUST understand that to be an effective leader, he/she must serve. John Maxwell shares his leadership philosophy as *"One life influencing another. This is the heart of leadership. One person casting vision. One person forging legacy, so that their influence incites the same passion in those they seek to lead. Afterall, people are our most valuable asset. [Affording] …you the power to impact those lives, to motivate teams, to transform organizations… We believe leadership is a process marked by constant growth."* (John Maxwell on Leadership, https://www.td.org/magazines/td-magazine/john-maxwell-on-leadership, by ATD Staff, February 8, 2013). Mentoring is the truest form of leadership any person can participate in. Leadership, in a nutshell, takes everything covered in the previous pillars and brings it into perspective for the mentor to understand their role in the mentor-mentee relationship. In the article, *Develop Leadership Skills with a Mentor,* (https://www.togetherplatform.com/blog/mentoring-develop-leadership-skills-with-a-mentor, by Matthew Reeves, August 1, 2021) the author says, *"Mentorship. Leaders learn through direct experience and the advice of others… mentors provide role models and guidance that future leaders can aspire to be like. Mentorship, in short, builds leadership skills."* The mentor's ability to see past their hopes, dreams, and desires to serve as a life or career guide to another person identifies within themselves their leadership qualities. The same qualities that will be modeled in front of the mentee as they learn how to navigate their journey called life. **Tony Dungy** shared in the *4 Essential Traits of a Mentor Leader,* (https://www.allprodad.com/4-essential-traits-of-a-mentor-leader/) *"In my life and career, I have seen all kinds of leaders. The ones who have had the greatest positive impact on my life are the select few who have been not only leaders, but also mentors. Here are four essential traits of a mentor leader to keep in mind:*

1. *Becoming a mentor leader is not rocket science. Leadership comprises of principles and skills that are accessible to anyone and everyone. They aren't necessarily intuitive, but they aren't terribly difficult, either.*

2. *Mentor leadership can be taught and learned; but in order to be absorbed, it must be practiced. The best way to evaluate leadership philosophies and find your own style is by testing them in action.*

3. *Mentor leadership focuses on developing the strengths of individuals. It might be in a narrowing way, such as building a specific skill, or more broadly focused, such as teaching employees to be proactive about meeting others' needs so they can better support the organization. Successful mentor leaders make the people they lead better players, workers, students, or family members and, ultimately, better people.*

4. *Mentor leadership works best when the ones being mentored are aware that the mentor leader has a genuine concern for their development and success. Those we lead will be more receptive if they believe we genuinely want them to succeed."*

As I was reading through Tony's essential mentor leadership traits, I thought about the many mentors I have had throughout my life and career, and how each of them instilled something in me I still use today. The same journey I took to get to where I am today, is the same journey mentors will take mentees to help them maximize the mentoring experience and take the skills they've gained, lessons they have learned and the experience that have totally changed their lives to become the best version of themselves possible. As Tony said, "*…this isn't rocket science…,*" it is an opportunity to give back and to impart knowledge into another person who helps them see beyond their limitations into the expansive world which is theirs to experience however they deem necessary.

ROLE MODELING

The article, *Positive role models and mentors have an important role to play in promoting pro-environmental behaviors,* (https://research.childrenandnature.org/ research/positive-role-models-and-mentors-have-an-important-role-to-play-in-promoting-pro-environmental-behaviors/, Prince, H.E., (2017). Outdoor experiences and sustainability. Journal of Adventure Education and

Outdoor Learning, 17(2), 161-171.) says, "*Social learning theory includes the idea that people learn behaviors by observing others. This theory supports the utilization of role models and mentors in educational programs designed to influence the behaviors of children and youth.*" The article goes on to say, "*Through role modeling, mentoring, and coaching, educators can also promote students' sense of empowerment and commitment to sustainability. Effective mentorship provides benefits for both the mentor and mentee. The mentee gains increased confidence and skill, while the mentor experiences renewed enthusiasm.*"

To better understand the role of the mentor and an important aspect of their mentor-mentee relationship, let's examine what a role model is. According to *Role Model vs. Mentor: Compare & Contrast*, https://study.com/academy/lesson/role-model-vs-mentor-compare-contrast.html, by Artem Cheprasov) "*A role model is an individual whose example, such as their behaviors or successes, are looked up to and imitated by others... Mentors are like personal role models. More formally, we can state that mentors are trusted individuals with more experience and wisdom than another person who helps guide that person with respect to a particular concern or desire. There is a personal, two-way relationship here. Mentors want to see you succeed, while role models may not even know who you are!* As I was reading this article, it became apparent that a mentor MUST choose to be a role-model and model the behavior, attributes and/or abilities of a leader in front of their mentee for them to observe it, internalize it and model it in their daily life. In the chapter on LEARNING, *I shared, "LEARNING only happens where we see the value in acquiring or obtaining the information for internal or external use. Sometimes the information is only valuable to you because of your own personal values and the accomplishments you desire for your life.* [It provides] *the freedom to make a decision that changed their perspective regarding the situation and make the decision that was the right one for them in that moment.*" Think about that for a moment! In the same way that a mentee determines which information offered by the mentor is valuable, the mentor must determine what information to share that will be of value to the mentee. That alone can change the mentee's perspective, behaviors and/or attitude toward life, school, their community, and the world. That's the power of mentors being a role model and leading their mentees by example. They take the best they have to offer and that is relevant in that moment. The mentor has the potential of impacting their mentee's life in a way that empowers and enables them to activate and model what they have observed and learned.

LEADERSHIP SKILLS/QUALITIES

Now that we have spoken about the mentors, let's talk about the information that will help the mentor equip and empower the mentee to step into the role of a leader as a result of participating in an effective and successful mentoring program. As we discuss leadership qualities, the mentor is to impart to the mentee keep in mind that "*…mentoring is a process for the informal transmission of knowledge, social capital and the psychosocial support perceived by the recipient as relevant to work, career or professional development; mentoring entails informal communication, usually face-to-face and during a sustained period of time, between a person who is perceived to have greater relevant knowledge, wisdom or experience (the mentor) and a person who is perceived to have less (the protégé or mentee).*" (*Develop Leadership Skills by Mentoring*, https://www.reliableplant.com/Read/29332/mentoring-develops-leadership, by Debbie Zmorenski, from excerpt by Bozeman, Feeney, 2007,)

1. **COMMUNICATION.** Having excellent communication skills is an essential leadership competency. The best leaders are skilled communicators who can communicate in a variety of ways, from transmitting information to inspire others to coaching direct reports. And you must be able to listen to, and communicate with, a wide range of people across roles, geographies, social identities, and more.

2. **TIME-MANAGEMENT.** Time has a monetary value today. Time-management requires a person to organize and prioritize tasks to be more effective with consideration to any competing priorities.

3. **CRITICAL THINKING.** Critical thinking is one of the topmost important skills required of successful leaders. Critical thinkers are intelligent decision makers, highly analytical and always rational. A

leader must be able to stand firm on his/her decisions. Because he/she is a critical thinker, it should be safe to assume that every decision he/she makes is well researched, objectively scrutinized and that all potential outcomes were assessed, and therefore, their eventual choice is the best course of action.

4. **RESPECT.** In today's society, there seems to be a misnomer that states ***to get respect, you must give respect.*** Although that may be the way of the world. It is not the sign of a good leader. A good leader gives respect understanding that by doing so, he/she is teaching others how to respect and treat them. Respect is inherent (*existing in something as a permanent, essential*). It is not about the absence of disrespect, but about how a leader can INFLUENCE (*authentically and transparently being able to convince people through logical, emotional, or cooperative appeals*) others while building and sustaining mutually beneficial relationships that are built on a foundation of RESPECT.)

5. **LEARNING AGILITY.** A leader who has learned the importance of being a life learner is one who learns from their mistakes and those of others, seek opportunities to grow while asking insightful and informative questions, and are open to hear other's opinions and feedback on relevant topics. This leader realizes that there are truly no failures in life, only opportunities to learn how to do something more efficiently and/or differently. This includes recognizing when new behaviors, leadership skills, and/or attitudes are needed and seeking opportunities to develop them.

6. **CHANGE MANAGEMENT AND INNOVATION SKILLS.** Change happens whether or not you want it to and being able to manage change in both your life and in business is essential when leading yourself and people. Wikipedia defines change management as a *collective term for all approaches to prepare, support and help individuals, teams, and organizations in making organizational or structural change.* Before change can occur, there must be some sign that change is needed. I think Oprah said it best, *"The greatest discovery of all time is that a person*

can change his future by merely changing his attitude." Think about that for a moment. Change happens every second of every day, whether or not we acknowledge it. It singularly can usher an individual into the next season of life or be the reason they are left behind because they refuse to accept and do what is necessary to manifest it in their life. This is an aspect of being a life learner (Learning Agility) especially when a leader recognizes "…*when new behaviors, leadership skills, and/or attitudes are needed and [seeks] opportunities to develop them.*" That's when genuine change happens!

7. **SERVICE-MINDED.** A servant leader feels responsible to help people learn and grow, feel purposeful, motivated, and energized, as he/she contributes to the betterment of the people and not merely selfish gain. He/She realizes this calling isn't about him/her but about the people! Simply put, servant leaders have the humility, insight, and courage to accept, acknowledge and understand that their greatest lessons have come from the people they interact with and/or surround themselves with. Leaders understand that as they accept their right to their views and/or opinions they must also do so with others simply because they are a member of humanity. A servant leader searches for opportunities to serve others with the understanding that before he/she can effectively serve anyone else, they MUST first be a servant to themselves. Malcolm X said, "*We can't teach what we don't know, and we can't LEAD where we can't* [or won't] *go.*" The following are some significant attributes of a service-minded leader (*6 Reasons Why Servant Leadership is Best,* https://www.rootinc.com/why-servant-leadership-really-works/, by Jim Haudan, October 26, 2020), however, we are only covering three reasons:

   a. ***Encourages others to think for themselves.*** It is not that we don't know. Sometimes we must talk it out to hear the solution as we speak. Which builds character, and confidence in ourselves and our abilities while helping us realize our place in the world.

b. ***Believe that all people are valuable and have something great to contribute.*** He/She refuses to believe that anyone has the right to or should throw people away as irrelevant. A service-minded leader builds trust with others from the care and genuine concern they show regularly. He/She believes in investing in people in the same way that others have invested in him/her.

c. ***Lives their life of service by asking one question: How may I help?*** This question empowers people to step up and say what they need help with. It *"…highlights the best in others, which will create far better results than if the leader dictated directions from their removed perspective. Servant leaders believe this approach reveals the untapped creative and performance capabilities of* [all] *people…"* (*Servant Leader as Change Agents - A Lean Journey*, by Tim McMahon, April 11, 2022, http://www.aleanjourney.com/2022/04/servant-leader-as-change-agents.html) This is necessary, regardless if the mentee is a youth, frontline employee, and/or community worker.

LEGACY

CHAPTER 7:
PILLAR: LEGACY

"Living your legacy is one of the best ways to feel happy while you journey through life." – Shyam Ramanathan

In the previous pillars, you have discovered the importance of living, loving, learning, laughing, and leading. All of which are necessary for you to live the legacy you want to leave the world, NOW. Benjamin Franklin once said, *"Don't put off until tomorrow what you can do today."* Living your legacy is one of the greatest gifts you can give to yourself, your family, the community, and the world, all at the same time. I know what you may think, *how can I do that?* The information in the LEGACY pillar will hopefully help you begin your journey of living the legacy you desire to leave the world. Yep, it begins with understanding, accepting, and believing what legacy is. Legacy is a living reflection of who you are. It is your story, unfolding in real time, and inspired by what makes life fulfilling.

Understanding what living your legacy entails begins with learning what legacy life, eulogy and resume values are. This basic understanding will begin the journey you are now on even though you haven't decided to live a life of legacy. As Maya Angelo said, "...*when you know better, do better.*"

Legacy Life: is a life that has a positive impact on someone else; makes conscious decisions each day; consciously focuses on the NOW moments that occur in life; happily, shares their time, attention, and essence with the ones they love and encounter daily; and spends time developing and completing their legacy life goals.

Eulogy Values: are what makes you stand for your highest values and by your deepest convictions; gives you the big picture of your life and gives you the impetus to create the life you desire. It is the virtues that show your inner light and inner character.

Resume Values: are the results of a life lived for external achievement. They are the skills and strategies you need for career success and build an external career that results in you living with an unconscious boredom, separated from the deepest meaning of life and highest moral joys.

BE ENTHUSIASTIC:
Get excited about your life! This is your opportunity to experience this world as it is. Genuine happiness draws others to you and allows you to build trusting and long-lasting relationships. Enthusiasm unlocks a life of substance and cheer; and be enthusiastic about life despite the obstacles each one faces.

BE GRATEFUL

Your attitude towards everything in life plays a greater role in how you like life and the opportunities you go after. Develop coping skills to view the world through a prism of abundance. Your attitude is the accurate barometer of how you experience your life. Your attitude sets the temperature for how other people see, relate, trust, and treat you. It can attract abundance and joy. When you're grateful your life has the ability to bring joy. The joy you experience while living your legacy is not based upon your outer success but your internal happiness. Your gratefulness is developed one small appreciative moment at a time. So, savor them and revere life.

ACCEPT YOURSELF

In the pillar on LIVING, we talked about discovering what you like, what you are passionate about. Identify those things you believe will bring you happiness and/or the drive you use to live your best life now. By doing so, this will help you live "...*thriving, vibrant, happy 'lives'.*" This gives you permission to live life well by doing things today that help you flourish in the moment, and in every day thereafter. Because this isn't something that is taught in the school or in some cultures, where it is socially acceptable. It must be introduced as an acceptable part of life for people to explore its necessity in their life.

Remember, your life is a gift! Accept the gift you have been given as the greatest present you have ever received. Live it by honoring it in the ways you talk about you, the love you lavish on it daily and the respect you freely give and receive. You are unique, no one else is equipped to be YOU. When you were created, the mold was broken. In an interview, Oprah Winfrey did in 2015, she shares "*What Mispronouncing 'Canada' on TV*" taught her. It taught her to always be who she is and show the essence of her truth. Otherwise, you will not be seen as being genuine. Accept the uniqueness that is you and live the legacy you want to leave your family, community, and world. Activate your gifts and talents and tap into your amazing strengths. If you don't do it, it will never be done. In the same way, you are not equipped to be anyone else.

"Legacy is every life you've touched." – Maya Angelou

CHARACTER: is the mental and moral qualities distinctive to an individual; strength and originality in a person's nature; a person's excellent reputation.

CHARACTER

Live your life according to your core values. Think about it this way: keep the end in mind and align all your activities to your highest values. Align your actions to what you want your life to stand for to ensure you live your legacy.

INSPIRE OTHERS

The way to inspire others is by being an influencer. One of the side effects of being a leader is inspiring others to tap into the best version of themselves and LIVE! In most cases, simply showing up as your authentic self enables, inspires, and empowers others to do the same.

ALWAYS RESPECT OTHERS

Live your life with one undeniable truth: respect is inherent! It shows that you value others as much as you value the gift that you are to the world. With that as a core value, always respect others. It frees you to continue living your best life while silently giving others permission to do the same.

DESERVING SUCCESS

Take positive action to overcome whatever fears you have developed over the years. It speaks to your self-love, acceptance, and the respect you have for yourself. Living your legacy means taking advantage of the opportunities available to you with the mindset that you are deserving of success. This is a tool to help you experience the success you desire. Believing in yourself means you believe you deserve success, and by acting out that belief daily, you put yourself in alignment with experiencing the success you want and deserve.

In the article, *Enlist In Your Purpose: Live Your Legacy Now*, the author, Heather Burgett, suggests each person seeking to live their legacy now to:

- ✓ Thrive through uncertain times.
- ✓ Stop making everything about YOU.
- ✓ Tap into your signature gifts.
- ✓ Recognize your sole reason to connect, interact, engage and be here for others – leads to unexpected opportunities for success.
- ✓ Be cognizant of this core belief: how I do one thing is how I do everything.
- ✓ Be a visionary who implements steps to create and effect change.
- ✓ Use life altering moments to fuel and/or energize you.
- ✓ Stretch, grow and move through challenges and unimaginable circumstances.
- ✓ Recognize the beauty in knowing YOU have the power to connect and support others.

BIBLIOGRAPHY

Why are there still so few Black executives in Amercia?,
https://www.usatoday.com/in-depth/money/business/2020/08/20/racism-black-america-corporate-america-facebook-apple-netflix-nike-diversity/5557003002/, by Jessica Guynn and Brent Schrotenboer, USA Today, August 20, 2020, updated February 4, 2021

Diversity Among Fortune 500 CEOs from 2000 to 2020,
https://whorulesamerica.ucsc.edu/power/diversity_update_2020.html, by Richard L. Zweigenhaft, Guilford College, January 2021

Closing the Gender Pay Gap: The gender pay gap has been stubbornly hard to close, but the tide may be turning, https://www.shrm.org/hr-today/news/hr-magazine/summer2019/pages/closing-the-gender-pay-gap.aspx, by Tamara Lytle, June 4, 2019

Closing the "Skills Gap." Here is how to do better,
https://www.mentorresources.com/mentoring-blog/closing-the-skills-gap.-here-is-how-to-do-better, by Andy Holmes, Jan 09, 2020

SWOT Analysis: Understanding Your Business, Informing Your Strategy,
https://www.mindtools.com/pages/article/newTMC_05.htm, by the Mind Tools Content Team

FREE 12+ Student SWOT Analysis Templates in Google Docs | Word | Pages | PDF, https://www.sampletemplates.com/business-templates/analysis/student-swot-analysis-template-pdf-word.html

Mentoring Program Sustainabiloity Plan Template,
https://idph.iowa.gov/Portals/1/userfiles/137/AmeriCorps%20Enrollment%20Forms/IDPH%20AmeriCorps%20Mentoring%20Program%20Sustainability%20Plan%20Template.pdf, First indexed on October 2012.

SWOT Analysis for Students, https://leverageedu.com/blog/swot-analysis-for-students/, by Team Leverage Edu, Updated on May 24, 202

SWOT Analysis: Questions for Personal SWOT,
https://www.civilservice.louisiana.gov/files/divisions/Training/Job%20Aid/Supervisor%20Toolbox/Questions%20for%20Personal%20SWOT.pdf

SUSTAINABILITY:

Mentoring Program Sustainability Plan,
https://idph.iowa.gov/Portals/1/userfiles/137/AmeriCorps%20Enroll
ment%20Forms/IDPH%20AmeriCorps%20Mentoring%20Program%2
0Sustainability%20Plan%20Template.pdf, October 2012.

Mentoring for the Sustainable Development Goals,
https://www.mentoring.org/blog/news/mentoring-for-the-sustainable-
development-goals/, by Mentor

Four Tips For Launching A Sustainable Mentoring Program,
https://www.ellevatenetwork.com/articles/6933-four-tips-for-
launching-a-sustainable-mentoring-program, by Molly Greenberg

Sustainability Planning and Resource Development for Youth
Mentoring Programs,
https://ojjdp.ojp.gov/library/publications/sustainability-planning-and-
resource-development-youth-mentoring-programs, Published September
2007.

APPENDIX

SAMPLE JOB DESCRIPTION FOR SENIOR MANAGER, MENTORING PROGRAM

POSITION TITLE:		CONTRACT LENGTH:
Senior Manager, Mentoring Program		
DATE:		**DATE OF LAST REVISION:**
JOB CODE	**PAY GRADE:**	**FLSA EXEMPTION STATUS:**

JOB SUMMARY

Directs operation and administrative functions for the Mentoring Program to streamline business operations, improve efficiencies, and advance the financial viability of the department. Administers through departmental managers, the interaction of the Mentoring Program services areas to maximize departmental solutions, revenues, and group performance.

MAJOR DUTIES & RESPONSIBILITIES

	List most important duties first
1.	Prepares plans and programmatic strategies for the Mentoring Program in the execution of major projects and various district and community initiatives.
2.	Assists the Academic Program Managers for the Mentoring Program in departmental financial activity, including quarterly and annual closeouts.
3.	Monitor implementation, provide programmatic adjustments, and coordinate resources to ensure successful completion of projects.
4.	Provides support and professional development for Academic Program Managers.
5.	Oversees the collection and presentation of performance and tracking data for the Mentoring Program directly under manager supervision.
6.	Manages the implementation of research-based strategies that support student learning.
7.	Creates reporting systems to regularly communicate progress to stakeholders and disseminate information on programs to families and community members.
8.	Collaborates with managers in other departmental duties assigned.
9.	Performs other job-related duties as assigned.

EDUCATION

Bachelor's Degree: Master's Degree preferred

WORK EXPERIENCE

5 to 7 years

Leadership experience in executing complex projects, classroom/school-based experience and/or community outreach experience working with diverse populations

TYPE OF SKILL AND/OR REQUIRED LICENSING/CERTIFICATION

Microsoft Office, Chancery
Office equipment (e.g., computer, copier)
Excellent organizational, communication, and engagement competencies
Bilingual (Spanish) skills preferred

LEADERSHIP RESPONSIBILITIES

Manages. Accomplish the majority of work objectives through the management of direct reports. Provides day-to-day direction to staff may become directly involved, as required, to meet schedules and resolve problems. Responsible for assigning work, meeting completion dates, interpreting and ensuring application of policies and procedures. Receives assignments in the form of objectives, with goals and the process by which to meet goals. Provides input to hiring, performance, and budget.

WORK COMPLEXITY/INDEPENDENT JUDGMENT

Work is substantially more complex, varied, and regularly requires the selection and application of technical and detailed guidelines. Independent judgment is required to identify, select, and apply the most appropriate methods, as well as interpret precedent. Position regularly makes recommendations to management on areas of significance to the department. Supervision received typically comprises of providing direction on the more complex projects and new job duties and priorities.

BUDGET AUTHORITY

Analyzes and interprets data and figures.

PROBLEM SOLVING

Decisions are made on both routine and non-routine matters with some latitude but are still subject to approval. Job is occasionally expected to recommend new solutions to problems and improve existing methods or generate new ideas.

IMPACT OF DECISIONS

Decisions have a moderate impact on the facility/department or division, causing increased satisfaction or dissatisfaction; producing efficiencies or delays; promoting or inhibiting personal intellectual or professional development; and/or contributing to financial gain or expense. Errors may be serious, usually not subject to direct verification or check, causing losses such as improper cost calculations, overpayment or improper utilization of labor, materials or equipment. Effect usually confined to the organization itself and is short term.

COMMUNICATION/INTERACTIONS

Collaborate and solve problems – works with others to resolve problems, clarify, or interpret complex information/policies, and provide initial screening/negotiations without approval authority. Interactions are typically with customers, senior level professional staff, and managers.

CUSTOMER RELATIONSHIPS

Regularly assesses and diffuses complex, and escalated customer issues. Takes personal responsibility and accountability for solving systemic customer service problems. Regularly explores alternative and creative solutions to meeting the needs of the customer within HISD's policies and guidelines.

WORKING/ENVIRONMENTAL CONDITIONS

Work is normally performed in a typical interior work environment, which does not subject the employee to any hazardous or unpleasant elements.
Ability to carry and/or lift less than 15 pounds.

SAMPLE JOB DESCRIPTION FOR MENTORING PROGRAM MANAGER

POSITION TITLE: Mentoring Program Manager		CONTRACT LENGTH:
DATE:		DATE OF LAST REVISION:
JOB CODE:	PAY GRADE:	FLSA EXEMPTION STATUS:

JOB SUMMARY

Assists the Senior Manager of the Mentoring Program to implement a program to increase the number of students who successfully attend and graduate from high schools with a focus on college or career readiness. Delivers ATM Project to students and works directly with students, parents, and school personnel to ensure that the goals of the program are met. Coordinates various Mentoring Program events and summer programs that supplement school-year programming.

MAJOR DUTIES & RESPONSIBILITIES

	List most important duties first
1.	Creates, organizes, orchestrates, monitors, and prepares plans/programmatic strategies for the school campus/Mentoring Program in the execution of major projects and various district and community initiatives.
2.	Assists the Senior Manager of the Mentoring Program in departmental financial activity, including quarterly and annual closeouts. Promotes the Mentoring Program at school sites and leads student recruitment for designated populations.
3.	Monitor implementation, provide programmatic adjustments, and coordinate resources to ensure successful completion of projects.
4.	Provides support and individualized assistance to students in the program throughout the graduation process.
5.	Oversees the collection and presentation of performance and tracking data for the Mentoring Program directly under manager supervision.
6.	Manages the implementation of research-based strategies that support student learning, including the coordination and delivery of summer programming, including special presentations, college and career supports, and leadership training workshops.
7.	Creates reporting systems to communicate their progress to stakeholders and disseminate information on programs to families and community members.

8.	Collaborates with managers in other departmental duties assigned to collaborate with teams to design, evaluate, and enhance programming and curriculum.
9.	Works with various departments and campuses to keep on track with project plans.
10.	Performs other job-related duties as assigned.

EDUCATION

Bachelor's Degree

WORK EXPERIENCE

3 to 5 years

Leadership experience in an academic setting, classroom/school-based experience and/or community outreach experience working with diverse populations

TYPE OF SKILL AND/OR REQUIRED LICENSING/CERTIFICATION

Microsoft Office, Chancery

Office equipment (e.g., computer, copier)

Excellent organizational, communication, and engagement competencies

Bilingual (Spanish) skills preferred

LEADERSHIP RESPONSIBILITIES

Level 2 - Work Leadership. Regularly provides project management or team leadership to a group of two or more employees but does not have formal supervisory responsibility. Leading and directing are restricted to monitoring work and providing guidance on escalated issues. Most of the time is spent performing many of the same duties they are leading.

WORK COMPLEXITY/INDEPENDENT JUDGMENT

Work is substantially more complex, varied, and regularly requires the selection and application of technical and detailed guidelines. Independent judgment is required to identify, select, and apply the most appropriate methods, as well as interpret precedent. Position regularly makes recommendations to management on areas of significance to the department.

PROBLEM SOLVING

Decisions are made with greater freedom and discretion, including recommendations that need approval on matters that may affect multiple departments across HISD. Job is frequently expected to recommend new solutions to problems, to improve existing methods/procedures/services and generate new ideas. May also review decisions made by other individuals on more routine matters.

IMPACT OF DECISIONS

Decisions that have a moderate impact to the facility/department or division, causing increased satisfaction or dissatisfaction; producing efficiencies or delays; promoting or inhibiting personal intellectual or professional development; and/or contributing to financial gain or expense. Errors may be serious, usually not subject to direct verification or check, causing losses such as improper cost calculations, overpayment or improper utilization of labor, materials, or equipment. Effect usually confined to the organization itself and is short term.

COMMUNICATION/INTERACTIONS

Collaborate and solve problems – works with others to resolve problems, clarify or interpret complex information/policies, and provide initial screening/negotiations without approval authority. Interactions are typically with customers, senior level professional staff, and managers.

CUSTOMER RELATIONSHIPS

Regularly assesses and diffuses complex, and escalated customer issues. Takes personal responsibility and accountability for solving systemic customer service problems. Regularly explores alternative and creative solutions to meeting the needs of the customer within HISD's policies and guidelines.

WORKING/ENVIRONMENTAL CONDITIONS

Work is normally performed in a typical interior work environment, which does not subject the employee to any hazardous or unpleasant elements.

Ability to carry and/or lift less than 15 pounds.

SAMPLE MENTOR OBSERVATION FORM

Program Manager: _____ Date: _____

School: _____ Start Time: _____

Observer: _____ End Time: _____

	Observation	Comments (on what is observed)
Directions: The evaluator uses this form to document informal observations. One form will be given to the program manager and one copy will be maintained by the evaluator for the entire evaluation cycle to document growth. **It is unlikely that all program manager performance standards would be documented during a single campus visit. In fact, an observation might focus on a specific standard.** Area **Standard Expectations:** Manager dresses in a manner that is appropriate for the job assignment, complies with campus or department procedures, arrives at work on time, and is punctual for scheduled meetings.	- Manager dresses in a manner that is appropriate for the job assignment and in a manner that reflects positively on the district. - Manager was expected to arrive at Sam Houston HS at 8am today. He reported to the campus at 9:15am.	Ensure your work calendar reflects the exact times at each location. Make sure you follow the schedule accordingly and inform your supervisor of any unexpected changes.
Seeks feedback in order to improve performance	- Manager was receptive to suggestions and valued feedback provided by the Senior Manager.	Work consistently on the implantation of the new student enrollment strategies shared by Senior Manager.
Planning and Organization: Manager determines departmental goals that align to the goals of the District, understands organizational matters, and aligns work accordingly by establishing effective processes, workflow, and integration with others.	- There is a total of 1 student and 3 mentors registered for the ATM project at this campus. - Campus Assistant Principal and College Coordinator were introduced as point of contact for ATM. They both described the program as highly effective.	* Be reminded that by April 18, 2019, you are expected to have a total of 25 students registered at this campus and 20 mentors in all your campuses combined. * Contact school staff, wraparound specialist, and school community counsel to help bring more mentors to this campus. * Consider the following strategies when recruiting new students: - Prepare enrollment package for the students to take home (Student and Parent Agreement Forms, Media Release Form, and Program Overview). Place all documents in an envelope and write the student's name on the back.

- Create a sign-in sheet to document the process (Student name, ID, Student/Parent Phone Number, Email). Have all your students to sign-in as they come.
- Introduce the program to prospective students and get them excited about participating.
- With students' input, develop a plan to assist them when asking their parents to sign the documents and bring them back to you the next day. Some students may prefer a text message, a phone call to parents, an email, etc. Do what you can before the end of the same business day to remind students and parents to bring the required paperwork the next day.
- Do your best to return to the campus the next day and follow up with the students regarding the permission slips. If you cannot return the next day, please identify a campus point of contact willing to assist you with the collection of the forms.
- Repeat this process as necessary and conference with the students until you meet the goal.

Promotes Highly Effective Mentoring Sessions	- Manager is currently facilitating mentoring sessions at the campus College Center. The space is adequate and conducive for learning.	Consider the use of the conference room in Room 2315 if additional space is needed as you grow the program on this campus.

SAMPLE MENTORING GUIDELINES AND AGREEMENT

MENTORING PROJECT FOCUS

The focus of the mentoring intervention is to provide each Tier 3 student assigned to a mentor who can provide ongoing support for the duration of their time in the district. This mentoring project will also contribute to the office of Social Emotional Learning's efforts to decrease recidivism in referrals.

SOCIAL AND EMOTIONAL LEARNING

Mentoring relationship is one intervention used to address recidivism; therefore, mentor status has been added to the referral data. This new data point can capture whether a student has an active or inactive mentor arrangement at the time of referral.

PROGRAM DOCUMENTS: The following have been identified as documents needed to formalize the mentoring program collaboration.

- Mentoring Agreement Contract
- Mentor Profile (electronic)
- Mentoring Introduction/Welcome PPT
- Mentor Program Guide
- Mentor Training Materials
- Mentoring Contact Log
- Mentee Transition/Follow-Up Plan

1. Establish Guiding Principles for the mentoring program. Helps to establish program expectations and marketing materials. This also helps in assessing how mentors and students are matched.
2. Use additional indicators such as attendance records to help support findings on recidivism rate.
3. Identify improved student outcomes that use a strengths-based approach. (e.g. self-efficacy, self-image, & student connectedness to adults/school).
4. Identify the measures to evaluate student success and include benchmarks (e.g., 30 days; 6 months; 1 year)

5. Explore multiple approaches to mentoring. This is not a one-size-fits-all effort. Should be open to innovative way to build transformative relationships with students.

Mentoring Project Core Objectives

- To build student self-reliance and resilience
- To build healthy attachments
- To improve positive connections to adults and peers in the school environment
- To enhance social, communication, relationship, and decision-making skills
- To maintain a connection, the mentor-scholar connection

Mentor Training & Networking

Every mentor who enters a partnership with the student will receive training in secure attachment theory. We recognize our mentor partners may have extensive knowledge and experience in connecting to at-risk youth, however it is imperative that a working framework is adopted and consistently shared among the partners in our program. Our trainings will provide awareness, knowledge, and strategies to foster positive relationship with students. Mentoring partners will be expected to engage in quarterly trainings throughout the year. CAMPUS leaders are committed to create successful mentoring connections between mentors and scholars. Training sessions will serve as an opportunity where mentors can share best practices and identify opportunities that address the challenges expected with this innovative approach.

Mentor-Scholar Matching Process

All mentors are required to complete a profile. That information, along with a photo, will be entered into a mentor database that will be shared with CAMPUS scholars. The purpose is to allow to involve our scholars in the matching process when appropriate. CAMPUS leaders will work directly with the scholar to facilitate a successful match. While there is no set timeline for the mentor matching process, the goal is for each scholar to have a mentor assigned prior to returning to their home campus.

Mentor-Scholar Bridge Out to Home Campus Process

Upon leaving the CAMPUS, each student should have a plan in place to continue working with their mentor/mentoring organization. Mentor or mentoring organizations might be required to collect follow-up data needed for the purpose of program evaluation.

Sample Mentor Program Contract

Mentor Expectations

1. To meet regularly with a scholar (see Mentor-Scholar Contact Log)
2. To monitor scholar's progress and identified goals
3. To notify campus leadership if unable to keep to scheduled meeting
4. To engage in the relationship with an open mind
5. To collaborate with campus leaders in identifying critical student needs
6. To keep (non-safety) conversations with scholar confidential
7. To seek assistance and ask for clarification when help is needed
8. To establish contact and maintain ongoing communication with scholar's family or identified support network

Acknowledgement of Forms (Please initial by each line)

____ I have read and understand the overall mission/vision of the Secondary CAMPUS and the Mentoring Program Objectives.

____ I understand my roles and responsibilities per the expectations identified above.

____ I understand that I am a part of a larger team of social, emotional support leaders assigned to my scholar

____ I have received a copy of the scholar expectations, Mentor-Scholar Questionnaire, and Contact Log

____ I have completed the mentor profile and submitted to the CAMPUS

____ I have read and understand the Mentor-Scholar Transition Outline

---

Mentor (Print Name):_____

Organization/Affiliation: _____

Signature: _____ Date: _____

SAMPLE MENTEE/SCHOLAR AGREEMENT

As a mentee/scholar with the Secondary CAMPUS Mentoring Project, I agree to the following:

1. To meet regularly with my campus mentor
2. To be on time for scheduled meetings
3. To notify the mentor if I cannot keep my weekly meeting
4. To engage in the relationship with an open mind
5. To accept assistance from my mentor
6. To keep discussions with my mentor confidential
7. To practice skills and behaviors taught to me by my mentor

Acknowledgement of Program Expectations (Please initial by each line)

____ I have read and understand the overall mission/vision of the Secondary CAMPUS and the Mentoring Program Objectives.

____ I understand what is expected of me as a scholar

____ I understand I should put forth an effort to practice new skills and behaviors

____ I know my mentor will continue to work with me even once I return to my home campus

Mentee (Print Name) _____

Signature: _____

Date: _____

Mentor-Scholar Initial Meeting Questionnaire & Strategies

Mentor	Mentee/Scholar
Questions you might ask…	Questions you might ask…
What can you tell me about you? What do you like to do for fun? What type of things are you good at? What makes you (proud/happy/excited)? What makes you frustrated or upset? What do you believe you need help with? What makes you scared? What are you looking forward to? Tell me about your family? How many siblings do you have?	What can you tell me about you? What do you like to do for fun? What type of things are you good at? What makes you (proud/happy/excited)? What makes you frustrated or upset? What do you believe you need help with? What makes you scared? What are you looking forward to? Tell me about your family? How many siblings do you have?
Mentor: These questions can be written on index cards for the scholar to ask of you. You may have to help prompt the initial discussion.	
Strategies you might use…	**Strategies you might share with your Mentee/Scholar**
<ul><li>Come Prepared. Learn what you can about your scholar before the initial meeting.</li><li>Talk about the big picture. What is your overall expectation? Why are you doing this work?</li><li>Discuss scholar's needs.</li><li>Ask questions and employ active listening.</li><li>Be clear about your goals. Make sure you explain what you can and cannot do.</li><li>Seek agreement on responsibilities.</li></ul>	<ul><li>How to prepare for a meeting</li><li>How to listen intently and ask questions</li><li>How to identify a need and set a personal goal</li><li>How to problem solve</li><li>How to use effective communication</li></ul>You might employ different approaches to help your scholar learn new skills and strategies. This could include direct lessons, modeling the behavior you want

• Set a timetable on an incremental basis. Make sure you can measure your goals with your scholar. • Agree on the next meeting time after every meeting. Provide options for days and times that work for your scholar. • Insist on confidentiality. Please also share your duty to ensure for the safety of your scholar. • Agree to be honest and candid. Communicate to your scholar your willingness to accept his/her feedback. Allow awkward exchanges to become teachable moments.	them to use, personal stories, family, or school meetings.

SAMPLE MENTORING PROGRAM TEAM

These are the individuals who are responsible for the mentoring intervention implementation. They are your primary point of contact through this partnership. _____ (xxx) xxx-xxxx; _____ (xxx) xxx-xxxx; and _____ (xxx) xxx-xxxx.

Sample Mentor-Scholar Contact Log

Scholar Name:	Mentor Name:	Mentor Phone #:
Scholar Home Campus:	Organization/Affiliation:	Total Contact Hours:

Using the log below, please describe the type of time spent with your scholar. Types of contact include (but are not limited to): one-to-one session; community outing; school meeting; family meeting. Please also briefly describe the nature of your contact. For example, if you met "one-to-one" for a session with your scholar, please state the overall object (i.e., goal setting).

Type of Contact:	Description:	Date of Contact	Total Time Spent

ACTION PLANNING FOR SCHOOL

PRINCIPALS	EMAIL	CAMPUS	Program Manager	FEEDER PATTERN SCHOOLS	MALE STUDENTS TOTAL	AFRICAN AMERICAN MALES	HISPANIC MALES	BOARD MEMBER

CULTURAL AWARENESS ACTIVITIES (PILLAR: LEARNING)

Self-awareness develops when a person recognizes who they are and their identity (age has no bearing in this instance) relative to the following:

- although they are aware of the differences, how you understand your racial and cultural identity plays a major part in understanding all cultures; and
- how you fit into a larger group centered around who supports your racial and cultural identity speaks to how you relate to yourself and others.

Activity 1:   Use magazines, ads and/or newspapers to find pictures that represent different cultures shown through their choice of clothing.

Activity 2:   Values Spectrum Activity/Conversation

Purpose: highlight the ways values and cultural norms intersect; this will help identify where your values fall on a continuum of different values.

Activity: Introduce the general concept of a continuum as a kind of a line within the room. Invite participants to stand on either side of the line based on the description or comments shared.

Scenario: You have entered a small business and the person in the store speaks and you return a salutation of your own with a smile. As you are reviewing the products they have for sale, you feel someone is watching you. You look up and see the person is watching you. You smile at them and keep looking around. After a while, you begin to feel irritated because they are following you around. You decide to leave, with the intention that you will never shop here again. (Ask participants how they would feel, if put in this same position? If they don't feel one way or another, stand to the right of the line. If they feel disrespected, stand to the left of the line.) [Once everyone has chosen a side, continue with the story:] As you are nearing the door, you hear another employee speak to the person staring at you say, "…*why are you at the cash register? You know you can't see anything since you left the eye doctor, and they dilated your pupils.*"

Debriefing: How would you handle the situation with the information you now have? (Tell the participants that they can change sides if they choose to or they can remain where they are.) After everyone has secured their spot on either side of the line, ask the group why did some people change sides? Or not?

THE FOUR COMPONENTS OF A SWOT ANALYSIS

A SWOT analysis is conducted to identify the strengths, weakness, opportunities, and threats to an individual or business. These are the four components being studied in a SWOT analysis. These four components are further divided into internal and external factors. Strengths and weaknesses are part of the internal factors, while opportunities and threats are part of the external factors.

Internal Factors:
These factors are those that can be changed and controlled by individuals or businesses, as it is something that they have in themselves that affects how they do things.

Strengths – This refers to the things that one is good at or where one is doing an excellent job. It could be any skill or talent that one can do, or something that they can learn and understand. Examples of strengths include job experience in a certain field, ability to communicate well using a different language, having a degree in a particular course, etc.

Weakness – It is the opposite of one's strengths, which means they are the things that one is not capable of doing or things they do poorly. This includes lack of work experience, lack of self-confidence, not able to communicate clearly, short attention span, etc.

External Factors:
External factors cannot be controlled as they are those things that happen around an individual or business that are caused by a natural occurrence or by another individual or business.

Opportunities – May also be referred to as the number of chances that one can take advantage of to achieve their goals or part of their goals. Examples of opportunities are joining networking events, being an alumnus of a certain university or school, new business openings, etc.

Threats – Threats are those things that may hold one down or pull one down if not determined and addressed immediately. Threats include lack of self-knowledge, not making any improvements at work or in school, failing to arrive on time for a job interview or business meeting, etc.

Before you even start with your SWOT analysis, make sure that you know each of its components and that you have prepared the needed questions to guide you through the entire process. The formal aspect of the chart is the same as in economic analysis: strong points (Strengths) are positive aspects that can be controlled from the interior and used in advantage and weak parts (Weaknesses) which are the negative ones that, by control can be minimized and/or improved. Regarding the external conditions which depend on the environment, opportunities (Opportunities) are positive external conditions, profitable, uncontrollable, and fears (Threats) are negative external conditions, obstacles, uncontrollable risks, the effect of which can be foreseen and avoided.

The personal SWOT analysis relevant criteria are:

a) Strengths:

- What do you do best?
- What are your positive traits?
- What distinct advantages do you have? (in terms of educational qualifications, work experience, networks, etc.)
- What is your greatest achievement?
- What resources do you have or have access to?
- What strategies do you use to reach your goals?
- What do other people see as your strengths?
- What type of resources do you have to invest in your career path?

b) Weaknesses:

- What tasks do you avoid doing because of a lack of confidence?
- What disadvantages do you need to work on?
- In which areas, you need more education or skill-based training?
- What personality traits do you believe are holding you back?
- What fears do you have that may hold you back?

- What are your negative traits or habits?
- What type of resources do you lack?
- In what areas do you need help in or more training or education?
- What racial or economic disparities do you experience?

d) Opportunities:

- What types of obstacles are you facing in your life, community, school, etc.?
- Are any of your strengths holding you back?
- Are any of your weaknesses preventing you from becoming successful?
- Are there are any obligations which are limiting your personal or professional development?
- What plans can you make today that will improve your future opportunities?
- How can you turn your strengths into opportunities?
- How can you turn your weaknesses into opportunities?

d) Threats:

- What obstacles do you face?
- Can any of your weaknesses prevent you from self-improvement and succeeding?
- Do any of your strengths hold you back?
- Do you have any obligations (home or otherwise) that may limit your personal development and succeeding?
- Are you competing with others for what you want?
- Are there events, actions and/or changes in your life or home that could threaten your future accomplishments and/or success?

What gives value to the SWOT analysis is that it can highlight opportunities that otherwise would not have been spotted. Thoroughness in completing the field destined for opportunities, preparing a comprehensive list of factors and their prioritization focuses attention on the most significant.

SWOT ANALYSIS TEMPLATE

Name: _____ Date: _____

(Examples: mentor role, mentee role, skills needed for a community service worker, quarterly self- review, etc.)

Think about how broad or narrow your analysis should be. It may be helpful to do multiple analyses. For example, if you are reviewing for a mentor and a mentee, you may want to make an extensive list of your strengths and weaknesses and list general opportunities and threats that pertain directly to their roles. Then will want to broaden the SWOT analysis and some very specific analysis based on your mentoring programs vision, purpose and/or goals.

Internal analysis sources (strength & weaknesses): self-analysis, what do you believe friends, family, and/or co-workers would say about you, personality quirks, and/or online personality assessments?

External analysis source (opportunities & threats): Any favorable situation, positive action/award that positively impacts you now or in the future. Traits that show your personality, abilities and/or talents in a positive light. Any unfavorable situations, behaviors, choices and/or decisions that are damaging now or could prove damaging in the future. Negative personality traits that have the potential of hindering your personal, professional and/or educational growth and development.

	HELPFUL	HARMFUL
	STRENGTHS	WEAKNESSES
INTERNAL ORIGIN Your personal strengths and weaknesses.	1. 2. 3. 4. 5. 6.	1. 2. 3. 4. 5. 6.
	STRENGTHS	WEAKNESSES
EXTERNAL ORIGIN External things that may impact you and/or your choices.	1. 2. 3. 4. 5. 6.	1. 2. 3. 4. 5. 6.

ABOUT THE AUTHOR

Dr. Kenneth D. Davis, Ed.D.

Dr. Kenneth D. Davis recently retired from the Houston Independent School District as their Executive Director of Equity and Outreach. Prior to this role, he was the Area Superintendent of the South Region, Assistant Superintendent of Equity and Outreach, Principal at Jack Yates High School, School Support Officer (principal supervisor), and Principal at Dowling (now Lawson) Middle School. He has had many titles and positions in the past 31 years, which began in the classroom molding and educating young minds.

Dr. Davis has a lengthy and successful track record in the business of education. Starting from the classroom he rose from classroom teacher to being selected as the campus teacher of the year, but the accolades were far from over. Dr. Davis became an assistant principal after his assistant superintendent noticed his flare and magic with teaching and 'encouraged' him to pursue a master's degree in educational administration. In doing so, he learned the role well and became a principal in the Lamar Consolidated Independent Schools within four years.

In the Lamar Consolidated Independent Schools, Dr. Davis moved the school from low performing to an Exemplary status with the support of an open-minded and hardworking staff. After two consecutive years, Dr. Davis was assigned to open a new elementary campus, McNeill, and that school also experienced Exemplary Campus performance. Dr. Davis had been nominated and selected as the Houston Area Alliance of Black School Educator's Teacher of the year, Principal of the Year twice) and awarded the National Distinguished Principal (NDP) for Texas Award, the highest honor an educator can receive.

Dr. Davis continues to share his knowledge and experience in supporting students by creating and developing districtwide mentoring programs like the Ascending To Men (ATM) and Resilient Outstanding Sisters Exemplifying Success (ROSES) that support students in need of mentorship as they matriculate through the educational system successfully and on to a career, college, and/or the military. He continues to be a positive and supportive force in education.

Dr. Davis credits his long-lasting career in education to building relationships, honoring education for all students, growing and developing teachers, and working to build strong instructional and visionary leaders. He works countless hours teaching at the University of Houston to guide instructional leaders to build reading skills for students that struggle and teaching the Equity in The Classroom course. Dr. Davis speaks and presents to future leaders across the country and has worked with several organizations to build and support future administrators through Columbia University and Birmingham City Schools. He mentors current principals, deans, assistant principals, instructional specialists, and teachers.